Turn, Turn, Turn... Please

Musings on cricket
and life by
Kerry
O'Keeffe

Turn, Turn, Turn... Please

ABC
Books

Published by ABC Books for the
AUSTRALIAN BROADCASTING CORPORATION
GPO Box 9994 Sydney NSW 2001

First published December 2007

ISBN 978 0 7333 2222 8.

Cover design by saso content and design
Internals set in 11.5/18pt Berkeley Book by Kirby Jones
Colour reproduction by Colorwize Studio, Adelaide
Printed and bound in Australia by Griffin Press, Adelaide

5 4 3 2 1

CONTENTS

INTRODUCTION

Surprise, surprise, a cricketer who has written a diary. Without being too apologetic, I'm hoping that this selection of days and events in my life will read a little differently to the 'I had muesli and fruit for breakfast, and "Gilly" batted very well today' approach, though there is a bit of that of course. I reckon sporting diaries are unfairly panned.

In an effort to expand on my initial offer, *According to Skull*, which dealt more with a chronological glimpse at my life, this is a collection of unrelated anecdotes, experiences and observations spanning thirty years. Each short story is self-contained; the book has not been written with any purpose of maintaining specific overall themes.

As a maverick, I have an inclination to drift ... in life ... in cricket commentary ... in print. This travail reflects the gypsy in my make-up.

It begins with my private thoughts during a cricket match in Yorkshire in 1975, where the winning of a television set consumed me for three days. Then, without any sense of order, I'm close to perishing in an aeroplane disaster. Perhaps I might have overreacted there ... but it was scary! And then there's my thoroughbred betting system. I felt at some stage it would afford me a grand lifestyle, but it has not quite realised its full potential. Still could, though, with the right mindset.

My offerings on the 2006–2007 Ashes whitewash, Australia's undefeated triumph at the 2007 World Cup in the Caribbean, and the analysis of the strengths and shortcomings of England and the West Indies in their 2007 Test series are opinions, and I hope they might be the subject of reader scrutiny during the 2007–2008 summer. There are a couple of financially testing days at the race track, as well as a description of the erratic performance of my horse, Skulla Crownie, a thoroughbred which I hope might some day win a Group One race.

Very much like *According to Skull*, this book is not intended to please the prose purist. My genuine endeavour is to provide light entertainment for the reader, not draw a nomination for a literary award. I want people to say 'It was a good read!' It is meant to draw guffaws and chuckles rather than plaudits for literacy. You can browse through the pages without a dictionary ... Speed readers will find it a doddle. Standing at the carousel at Perth Airport a couple of years ago, I was approached by a middle-aged fellow dressed in a tweed jacket and moleskin trousers. The conversation went like this:

'Skull ... enjoyed your book!'
   'Oh, thanks ... it's not difficult to read.'
   'Bloody oath, it's not ... I got through it on the trip over.'

At this stage I'm hoping he's about to tell me he boarded the jet in Auckland. Nervously I ventured:

'Where did you come from,?'

'Adelaide.'

As I said, I don't write long books!

IN PURSUIT OF A
TELEVISION SET

It is mid-summer in northern England. I am in the heart of the cotton city of Blackburn, playing Lancashire League cricket as the overseas professional for East Lancashire. I'm having a rather good season and I'm the fittest I've ever been. Three or four times a week I link up with a marathon runner called Dave Walsh and embark on gruelling fifteen-kilometre runs around the outskirts of this sprawling town. I've shed about ten kilograms in weight and am in peak condition every weekend for East Lancashire.

An invitation has come from Derek Robins to play in a match against the Yorkshire County team. I played for Derek a few years previously and enjoyed the occasion. His matches are very competitive and although not regarded as first-class fixtures there is an edge to the encounters. Traditionally Derek assembles a team whose members will enjoy each other's company and can play a little bit as well.

I drive to Harrogate, a small English village in west Yorkshire, on the morning of the game. The summer of '75 has been relatively dry and the pitch looks quite bare when I enter the ground. I will be in good hands over the next few days as Brian Close, my former Somerset captain, is to lead us, and I know a few of the others in my team, notably Ian Botham, Geoff Howarth, Geoff Miller and the late Graham Roope. The match begins, we win the toss and go in to bat—a good move.

I am a bit of a television fanatic but this summer I have a problem. I am staying at the Blackburn YMCA during my stint with East Lancs. I have a single-bedroom apartment. You can just squeeze a bed and a basin in it. There is no toilet and the showers are communal. The only television set at the Y is downstairs next to the dining room.

My fellow YMCA lodgers are students from all over Europe and Africa. There are Swedes, Finns, Greeks, Nigerians and Kenyans. It is a great mix and we all get on well though very few of them can speak much English and none know about cricket. I like eating with them at meal times but can never get near the television set as they watch endless documentaries on BBC2. Most of my weekday nights are spent in my room reading or writing letters back home. I yearn for my own television set—a simple portable that I could prop up in my room and watch to my heart's content. How could I get one? I'm an impoverished professional cricketer staying at a hostel; the price of a portable television set is beyond me.

As luck would have it, the Man of the Match for Yorkshire v. DH Robins's XI is to receive a brand new £150 portable television set with antenna. I saw it on the trophy cabinet as I walked into

'Beefy's' social doctrine is
'go hard or go home!'

the Robins dressing-room. I would kill for that television set, but cricket is a team game so I can't let my selfish ambitions be too naked. Our opening batsmen are Geoff Howarth of New Zealand and Jimmy Love of Yorkshire. They prosper against what was a weakened Yorkshire attack; rather fortunately, the great Geoffrey Boycott wasn't playing—that was a plus for everybody.

Howarth and Love went along swimmingly on a benign pitch. Love made ninety-five before being stumped off Phil Carrick, a left-arm orthodox spinner who was turning the ball despite not enjoying a reputation as a legitimate tweaker—good signs for me and the television set. Clive Rice of South Africa is in next. He is an all-rounder who would have played tremendous Test cricket at his peak yet, because of their international ban, was condemned to display his professional skills in England and elsewhere.

Batting at three he looks in tremendous form, holding the bat upright and slapping anything overpitched through extra cover. Eventually he is bowled by Arnold Sidebottom for sixty-three.

Close failed—out for four caught slogging one up in the air off Carrick. Roope comes in and in partnership with Ian Botham our total is rattling along. Roope was one of the best catchers I've ever seen throughout my career, a real spring-heeled jack in the slip cordon—his years of goal keeping for Corinthian Casuals sharpened his reflexes. Perhaps he should have played more Tests but he and a youthful Botham, who made forty, were giving our momentum a real boost.

I am listed to bat at number seven and I am in with the total on 283. 'Roopey' and I are in partnership and I'm enjoying

A youthful Ian Botham in relaxed mode

myself. My batting has come a long way because my fitness levels are so high, and I am working the ball through extra cover, whipping it off my pads. I feel comfortable. There's nobody really quick in the opposition. Sidebottom is honest, Carrick is accurate and Geoff Cope, a seasoned bespectacled off spinner whose right elbow at release made Murali's arm look fused, is operating and giving me width. I am slapping him through point. I have a polyarmour bat which is just a cannon—I love this bat, I sleep with this bat. When you haven't got a television in your room you need a good bat! At times in my room at the YMCA I just clean that bat. It stands next to the bed and often I wake up and play a shot with it. Today, every time I look to punch the ball I find a gap and the boundary. Eventually when Closey declares we have a total of 404 for eight down and I am sixty-five not out. Okay, that's at least the antenna of my television set.

Yorkshire is batting on the second day and Barry 'Bart' Stead is bowling well. Bart is a left-arm seamer who bends the ball back in. He looked sixty when he was twenty and he died young. Bart was never here for a long time, he was here for a good time. He smoked for England and drank for Great Britain. He was such a character! This day he removed both openers cheaply.

Clive Rice bowls a few overs but on this sluggish surface there is nothing much in it for Ricey. I'm pleased with that because after his first innings of sixty-three he was an early contender for man of the match.

Miller is bowling off spin and not looking too threatening. Closey has thrown me the ball. At once I'm turning it rather a long way. This was a pitch I wanted to take all around the world. The Yorkies have never had a history of playing leg spin well and

I am inducing leading edges to cover, bowling people through the gate, and eventually getting them to chip back to me as they looked to work through the leg-side.

In between times Carrick is hitting me for boundaries, as is Peter Squires who had come in at number three and did well for sixty-four. This ground is lightning fast and whenever I erred in length or line I paid with a boundary. Nonetheless a return of 5–86 off twenty overs is worthy of leading the team off the field. I'm ahead in the Man of the Mah reckoning. Love, Roope and Rice are in a pack behind me.

We're batting again. Rice and Love are already into the twenties but Closey declares before either of them has a chance to play a significant innings. I don't bat in the second dig.

The Yorkshiremen are set 359 to win on the last day. The pitch is already showing signs of wear. Carrick and Cope have turned prodigiously.

After multiple scotches prior to the final day, Closey says to me, 'Kerry you bowl that funny stuff. I'm going to give you a long bowl on the last day—don't let me down, lad.' No problems, captain! I've got one hand on the television set. A match-winning innings from a Yorkshireman and I'm dead, however, and it would be in my interests if Rice, Botham or Roope don't take too many wickets. Isn't cricket selfish on occasions?

On the final morning I have problems. Barrie Leadbeater is crunching boundaries off everybody including myself. I'm in trouble. Leadbeater is going to get Yorkshire across the line here and I'm going to have to watch documentaries in the common room for the rest of my stay in Blackburn. My spinning finger is bleeding courtesy of those twenty overs in the first innings, though I'm impervious to pain at this stage—it's all about the television set.

Almost at once Sidebottom chips one straight back to me for a caught and bowled. Carrick goes for a cow shot and loses middle stump. Roope at slip holds Graham 'Moonbeam' Stevenson and I have three wickets. Rice has come on and got two from the other end. Damn it. Bugger those South Africans. If he gets five I'm dead!

There are three to go. It will serve me best if Bart comes back and he duly does so and on cue gets a wicket. Just two left now. There's blood all over my fingers. Rice keeps asking the captain to bring him on again—he wants that TV set as well. Stuff him. Bloody South Africans, they're always after the booty.

Closey looks at my hand, 'Okay lad, you've got three wickets, I'll just let the quicks clean up.'

'No, Brian, please, it's okay,' I plead.

'But there's blood on the ball, lad,' he says.

'I don't care, I'll rip these last two out for you,' I declare.

I'm into my twenty-fourth over. I'm tired. Apart from the bleeding finger I'd been on the drink the previous night with Botham, Howarth and Bart. I'm dehydrated and I can hardly walk. There are two wickets available. We're going to win. Leadbeater is out for 110. It's a century in a losing team. I've got eight wickets in the match so far, on top of my runs. I've almost got that set. Closey keeps me on. I'm wiping blood off the ball with a towel. I'm bowling dross.

Cope, although wicketless during the game, is slogging me. This bespectacled twig of a man is raining on my parade and keeps hitting me for six. Closey has signalled for Rice to warm-up. He already has two wickets, if he gets four for the innings, I'm dead! Suddenly Howard Cooper goes for a big swing and nicks my leg break to slip and Love catches a blinder—I've got four—one to go.

By this stage I've got no skin on my index or middle finger at all, the ball is resting against raw bone. Yorkshire still needs another hundred and Cope is thirty-two not out. He's trying to get them over the line. He launches into another cow shot. Bart is at deep mid wicket. He's the worst catcher in the team and he was on the whisky last night till five am. I'm thinking that he's going to palm this for six. Closey's going to take me off and Rice will get the last wicket and the television set. Bart has lunged to his right, the ball has struck him on the wrist, then the mouth and as he tumbled it's fallen into his considerable midriff where he grasps it with both hands. The match is over. I have 5–76. The Robins XI has won by ninety runs.

Now for the presentations.

Everybody is shaking my hand and I'm apologising for the blood. I'm standing there cradling a can of Yorkshire bitter beer. The captains are thanked and presented with gifts for competing and it's time now for the Man of the Match. There's some shuffling. Will Leadbeater get it? There are a lot of Yorkshiremen on the presentation dais. Will Rice get the sympathy vote for being South African? Robins is a known South African sympathiser. All sorts of thoughts are racing through my head. Roopey fielded like a genius and bludgeoned seventy-eight in the first innings. Love got ninety-eight and twenty-four to set up the run chase—another Yorkshireman. Am I going to fall victim to

Graham Roope was one of
the best catchers I've ever
seen, and a fair bat, too

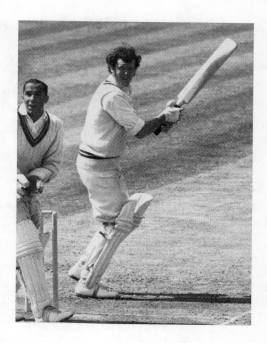

the Yorkshire bias? I've got three more months in the country—I can't possibly watch one more documentary.

The President of Yorkshire then announces, 'And the Man of the Match, please give him a round of applause, is from'—Australia, please say Australia—'Australia, Kerry O'Keeffe'.

Yes! Thank you! And he lifts the television set and presents it to me. I stagger off to put it in the car and then return to celebrate with my team-mates over copious amounts of Yorkshire bitter.

I've got my television set. I drive back to the YMCA, it's after midnight. The night watchman lets me in. He thinks I've pinched what's under my arm. I race up to my room and assemble it, put up the antenna and switch it on. Yes, there's a documentary on, but I don't care—it's my television set. I can change channels without seeking approval from anybody.

Thank you Derek Robins. Thank you Yorkshire for not being able to play leg breaks. Thank you Brian Close for disregarding the blood on the ball and keeping me on. I enjoyed the last three months at the YMCA despite shared showers, crap food and an inability to discuss any cricket at the dining room table—I had my TV.

Yorkshire v. DH Robins's XI

DH Robins's XI first innings		Runs	Balls	Mins	4s	6s
GP Howarth	c Bottomley b Sidebottom	35				
JD Love	st Bottomley b Carrick	95				
CEB Rice	b Sidebottom	63				
*DB Close	c Leadbeater b Carrick	4				
GRJ Roope	b Robinson	78				
IT Botham	c Leadbeater b Carrick	40				
KJ O'Keeffe	not out	65				
DJ Brickett	b Robinson	1				
G Miller	run out	5				
+A Long	not out	5				
B Stead	did not bat					
Extras		13				
Total (8 wickets, declared, 100 overs)		404				

Fall of wickets: 1–88, 2–201, 3–201, 4–217, 5–283, 6–346, 7–348, 8–365

Yorkshire bowling	Overs	Mdns	Runs	Wkts	Wides	No-Balls
Robinson	20	1	86	2	–	2
Cooper	16	3	62	0	–	1
Sidebottom	19	4	43	2	–	–
Carrick	25	2	91	3	–	–
Townsley	6	2	19	0	–	1
Cope	14	1	90	0	–	–

Yorkshire first innings		Runs	Balls	Mins	4s	6s
B Leadbeater	b Stead	43				
RAJ Townsley	c Brickett b Stead	6				
PJ Squires	c Close b O'Keeffe	64				
A Sidebottom	run out	24				
GB Stevenson	c Brickett b O'Keeffe	16				
P Carrick	c Brickett b O'Keeffe	50				
*JH Hampshire	c Roope b Close	7				
HP Cooper	b O'Keeffe	1				
GA Cope	c and b Stead	0				
AL Robinson	c and b O'Keeffe	14				
+SM Bottomley	not out	0				
Extras		13				
Total (all out, 75.1 overs)		238				

Fall of wickets: 1–14, 2–105, 3–124, 4–148, 5–168, 6–177, 7–193, 8–194, 9–213, 10–238 (75.1 ov)

DH Robins's XI bowling	Overs	Mdns	Runs	Wkts	Wides	No-Balls
Stead	16	5	38	3	–	–
Brickett	10	5	12	0	–	4
Rice	9	3	22	0	–	1
Miller	12	3	43	0	–	–
O'Keeffe	20.1	7	86	5	–	–
Botham	4	0	5	0	–	–
Close	4	1	19	1	–	–

DH Robins's XI second innings		Runs	Balls	Mins	4s	6s
GP Howarth	c Bottomley b Sidebottom	24				
JD Love	c and b Carrick	24				
CEB Rice	c Bottomley b Carrick	27				
GRJ Roope	not out	37				
IT Botham	not out	33				
G Miller	b Townsley	15				
*DB Close	did not bat					
KJ O'Keeffe	did not bat					
DJ Brickett	did not bat					
+A Long	did not bat					
B Stead	did not bat					
Extras		8				
Total (4 wickets, declared, 51.1 overs)		168				

Fall of wickets: 1–35, 2–52, 3–91, 4–97

Yorkshire bowling	Overs	Mdns	Runs	Wkts	Wides	No-Balls
Robinson	5	3	10	0	–	–
Stevenson	1	0	4	0	–	–
Sidebottom	9	1	28	1	–	–
Cooper	9	4	11	0	–	–
Carrick	13	1	46	2	–	–
Cope	4.1	0	13	0	–	–
Townsley	10	1	48	1	–	2

Yorkshire second innings		Runs	Balls	Mins	4s	6s
B Leadbeater	c Long b Rice	110				
RAJ Townsley	c Long b Rice	16				
PJ Squires	c and b Roope	12				
A Sidebottom	c and b O'Keeffe	13				
GB Stevenson	c Roope b O'Keeffe	1				
P Carrick	b O'Keeffe	6				
*JH Hampshire	c Howarth b Stead	8				
HP Cooper	c Love b O'Keeffe	6				
GA Cope	c Stead b O'Keeffe	32				
AL Robinson	not out	14				
+SM Bottomley	run out	0				
Extras		26				
Total (all out, 83.4 overs)		244				

Fall of wickets: 1–41, 2–74, 3–109, 4–123, 5–128, 6–138, 7–154, 8–226, 9–230, 10–244 (83.4 ov)

DH Robins's XI bowling	Overs	Mdns	Runs	Wkts	Wides	No-Balls
Stead	15	5	19	1	–	–
Brickett	6	1	14	0	4	3
O'Keeffe	26.4	4	76	5	1	1
Botham	2	1	4	0	1	–
Rice	11	7	18	2	–	–
Roope	9	2	16	1	–	–
Miller	5	0	29	0	–	–
Close	9	1	42	0	–	–

Source: Courtesy of cricketarchive.com

CONNAUGHTING WITH IMRAN KHAN

The picturesque Sydney University Oval No. 1 is the venue for a pre-Christmas District club cricket round. On this day the students are locked in battle with North Sydney. The Sydney Uni overseas professional for the summer is Imran Khan, the princely champion all-rounder from Pakistan. He has been engaged to play Sheffield Shield cricket for New South Wales and it seemed a perfect fit, having come from Oxford University in England, for him to join the club that represents the most prestigious university in this fair city. Imran is a good club man, he gets on well with his fellow players and gives 100 per cent in every match.

In the previous District match the Pakistani experienced the Australians' sensitivity when he battled with the University of New South Wales. He and his Sydney University team-mates were dismissed for just 120 chasing 160. Six of their batsmen were judged lbw, including former Test opener John Dyson and

Imran himself. The umpire who adjudicated on all six lbw decisions happened to be the father of the Sydney University batsman who had been surprisingly relegated to second grade for this match. Dad was having none of this and took his vengeance out on his son's former team-mates. Imran, one of his victims, was given out lbw to a ball which pitched some three feet outside the off stump and struck him on the thigh guard. He took it as nobly as any prince could.

The overseas star's next match was this two-day affair against North Sydney. University had been bowled out for 180-odd on the first day. In reply North Sydney reached 3–110 at lunch on this, the second Saturday and were in a very strong position to take the first innings points.

During his sojourn with New South Wales Imran was being accommodated at the Connaught, an upmarket apartment block

'See you next week boys.' After winning the match Imran Khan roared off, the blonde in the passenger seat

overlooking Hyde Park in central Sydney. Rents at this high-rise complex were far beyond the reach of most professionals. Imran entertained royally on the fourteenth floor and did not want, from all reports, for female company. 'Immie' was, to quote a team-mate, 'as Aussie as', though he stopped short of downing schooners of beer at the end of every match.

This day at the university oval a delicious blonde is perched high in the stands of this grand old ground throughout the morning session—and she only has eyes for the Khan boy. At the lunch break, with Sydney University's fortune hovering on a knife edge, the radiant beauty descends from on high, grabs Imran's hand and they waltz towards the car park. His team-mates think he has just ducked out for a quick sandwich in the park—a wrong assumption. That theory is immediately torpedoed as his late-model, bright red sports car accelerates out of the University car park bound for the Connaught—you get more than lunch with Imran!

The lunch break completed, there is no sign of Imran as Sydney University takes the field with only ten men. The North Sydney total mounts slowly, and still there is no sign of the Pakistani. The captain at the time, Michael O'Sullivan, is less than impressed. North's hopes of victory have risen sharply with the opposition's star bowler not on the field—and presumably expending energy his captain would require for a post-lunch bowling blitz.

Thirty minutes after play has resumed the red sports car re-enters the car park and Imran discreetly slips onto the field at deep fine leg. Within an over or so a wicket falls to make North Sydney 4–140, a tantalising forty-one runs short of victory with six wickets in hand.

As the players gather to celebrate the fall of wicket there is uneasiness among the team. Imran approaches from his boundary position, walks up to Captain O'Sullivan and, in his best baritone announces, 'I am ready to bowl now, captain.' Without hesitation the skipper throws him the ball and says, 'All right. I don't care what you've been up to, but we've just got to win this match.'

Graham Spring, a fine District player who has been capped by New South Wales on the odd occasion, is spearheading the North Sydney charge to victory. Imran hands his cap and jumper to the umpire and there follows the most withering spell of fast bowling seen at the ground for years. Consecutive bouncers strike Spring on the shoulder before middle and off stump are picked out of the ground by a searing yorker. Four more wickets fall to Imran for just two runs in his deadly spell. His team-mates embrace him at every wicket—5–3 in five overs and the match is Sydney University's by twenty runs.

Imran proudly leads his team off the field to a rapturous ovation from fellow players and support staff. After congratulations from the Chairman and the Sydney University Chancellor, Imran is at the door of the dressing-room with his kit under his arm. 'See you next week, boys' is his parting remark as he heads towards the car park. The red sports car again ignites and roars away from the university—the blonde back in the passenger seat. You can be sure the road leads back to the Connaught.

There is a strong body of support for 'connaughting' to be added to our language to describe such midday dalliances. And the Pakistani all-rounder could take full credit for its entry. What a champion. What a performance. What a way to do lunch!

SATURDAY, 19 JULY 1997

ANSETT AIR DRAMA—
A NEAR-DEATH ESCAPE

Whenever I travel by plane these days I always give the flight attendants my undivided attention when they demonstrate the safety drill. I wish my fellow passengers did the same. Most simply bury their heads in newspapers or magazines, oblivious to the tips that may result in some semblance of order should there be an emergency. I watch, however, because of past experience. I have witnessed the disorder of mid-air drama firsthand.

My chilling incident occurred one balmy Brisbane Saturday morning in 1997. The carrier that fateful day was Ansett Airlines, which not long afterwards went into receivership.

Twilight periods of any career can be difficult. Today was not to be my finest hour. I'd stayed a couple of days in Brisbane with my friend Andrew 'Slacky' Slack. We'd attended a rugby league match the previous evening at Lang Park and had played golf that afternoon. I was in buoyant spirits; Slacky had been a great host.

My friend Andrew 'Slacky' Slack was captain of the Wallabies during their 1984 Grand Slam triumph. But a true Queenslander, he was pretty unsympathetic about my mid-air drama

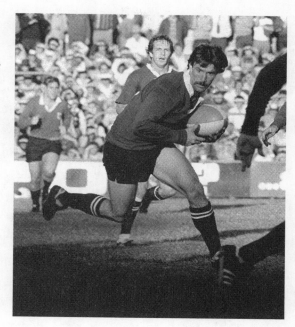

His sporting pedigree is sound. He captained the Wallabies in their 1984 grand slam triumph under the coaching of Alan Jones. While a number of people seem to be eager to condemn Alan Jones, I've never heard Slacky say anything untoward about the man. 'Pick and stick' is a Jonesism, and Slacky is a staunch apostle. He dropped me at the airport to catch the first flight out on Saturday morning, and then went on to have his 6.30 am game of golf at the prestigious Brisbane Golf Course. I bade him farewell and apologised that I couldn't accept his invitation to join him as I needed to get home to my family.

There was nothing unusual about my pre-flight routine: I had raisin toast and coffee while I perused the Brisbane newspapers.

I am a nervous flyer. Traditionally I do not like the first flight of the day—I figure the engines are cold and anything untoward of a terrorist nature that is going to happen would have been put in place overnight, if you know what I mean.

I'm towards the front of the plane, which in itself is unusual. Normally I'm back with the cattle but somehow I've jagged a seat inside the top ten. Seat 4B to be precise. I'm going to enjoy the pampering in business class. A representative rugby league team that had played the previous night are on board. I'm not certain of their exact title but there were liberal splashes of green and gold on their tracksuits and there was more than a hint that they'd won the previous evening. Consequently, their mood was bullish and it was obvious they were going to get up to some high jinks on this short hop to Sydney. Still, I was tired from two days of racing around Brisbane so all I wanted was an hour and a half to sleep.

The plane takes off. There isn't a cloud in the sky and I am relaxed. I love this sort of flying day. But we are 1000 feet or so over Moreton Bay when there is a thunderous bang from the back of the plane. It shakes the young footballers up. They had mimicked the flight attendants doing their routine—but the explosion concentrates their minds. An eerie silence engulfs the plane.

The captain is on the loudspeaker immediately: 'Would the flight attendants make their way quickly to the front of the aircraft. We have an emergency.'

A sighting of Paris Hilton reading a Bible would have had the same numbing effect on the cabin.

Call me a scaredy-cat, but I don't like any mid-air emergency when I haven't got a parachute! No need to tell Houston we have a problem. I just had to look at the faces of the flight attendants—I've seen Pakistani tailenders facing Dennis Lillee look more comfortable. Chopper Reed would have advised us to 'harden the f*** up', but the whole plane is crapping itself.

The Captain is on the loudspeaker again. 'We have an emergency. There is no reason to panic. We will be returning to Brisbane Airport at once. Please ensure that seat belts are fastened, and when we do touch down I'm ordering everybody to evacuate the aircraft via the emergency chutes and run 200 metres from the plane.' These are riding instructions even David Beckham would have understood.

Nobody says a word as the stricken airship makes a slow loop of Moreton Bay. There is a smell of petrol and a slight whiff of smoke. These are not smells I particularly like when I'm hovering a long way from the ground, travelling at several hundred kilometres an hour and feeling helpless. I prefer the whiff of salmon and chardonnay.

As we are making our emergency landing I see ambulances racing along on both sides of the runway. Potentially, this is like the clerks of the course attending to a jockey after the whole field of thoroughbreds has trampled over his defenceless body. There are fire engines as well, one of which runs into a ditch. For God's sake, I was hoping for a little more precision from the hired help.

The touchdown is laboured, as you may expect, but as the brakes are applied we are still racing along the runway. I am extremely nervous. I've never been in a life-threatening emergency—oh, except when forced to open the batting against Michael Holding and company in World Series Cricket.

We come to an abrupt halt and the emergency chutes are opened. Curiously, there is a measure of calm inside the plane.

The instructions from the flight attendants are to get up quietly and make our way to the emergency exits.

The Japanese tourists are oblivious to our situation and reach into the overhead lockers looking for cameras to capture our final moments. The fellow next to me says, 'Me take photo'. It would be difficult to take the photo with my elbow in his jaw. This was not the time for photos, you bloody fool, it was time for getting the hell outa there.

The first passengers are sliding down the chutes. There's not much conversation other than the Japanese bickering because they can't capture the moment on celluloid. I'm about the fifth person down the first chute on the right of the plane. I explain to the flight attendant who is about to make me slide that the chute is slit. She looks and notices that it has a gaping hole down the bottom. It appears that we should have removed our shoes. It's in the drill after all—or is it? Nobody paid any attention. Everybody still has their shoes on and so one of the first evacuees must have picked up a sharp object on their shoe and slit the chute, whereupon everybody who follows falls through onto the concrete tarmac.

I slide down the chute, hit the tarmac and execute the advice of the captain and run for my life. Some media men who'd covered the rugby league match the previous evening are on their mobiles, dialling into commercial radio gardening shows to report from the scene of the life-threatening drama at Brisbane Airport. I don't think mobile phones are really what is called for, given that the situation all round is inflammatory. Still, we are the news of the day!

I've had no time to stretch the hamstrings for my 200-metre sprint away from the aircraft, but I'm making my way quickly anyway. Fear can add yards to a man. I'm passing old people. A lady in her seventies is doing it tough, she's shortening stride in front of me. I get level with her, she grabs her chest and explains sensitively, 'Bad heart.' I'm accelerating, and as I pass her my comment is, 'Bad luck.' In these sorts of emergencies it's every man for himself—selfish, I know, but potential plane explosions tend to ignite self-interest in humans.

I'm around 200 metres from the plane now. We're all huddled in a semicircle. The radio men are on their phones explaining live-to-air to the gardening people how they were almost killed. A Japanese man has managed to grab his camera and is madly clicking.

Next moment a mini bus appears to take us back to the terminal, and we're all sitting there somewhat shell shocked when the driver says, 'Wow, what a sight. The flame out the back of your plane must have been 100 metres long. It looked spectacular.' Calming words indeed from the bussie. Just what you needed to know—that you could've gone up in flames that far up in the sky.

Within minutes we're back at the terminal. Ansett has provided tea and bikkies. Nice of them, although at the time I would have favoured a Scotch. Ice is being distributed to those who have fallen on the tarmac. Statements are being taken.

I ring Andrew Slack to ask him how his short game is and also to contrast how golf is so much less life-threatening than air travel. He dismisses my call as yet another New South Welshman overreacting.

We're herded towards an area where an Ansett official addresses us and apologises for the plane almost blowing up, or euphemisms to that effect. I move on quickly. We're dispersed onto an international flight. It's bigger than our faulty bird—it looks safer. And eventually my trip to Sydney is completed.

To this day I'm nervous on planes. While the flight attendant is doing the drill I count how many steps there are to the emergency exit. I'm mindful of how to blow up my life jacket. I know it's under the seat. I know where the whistle is. And I wish that she'd add that all shoes must be taken off. And for you tourists, an emergency is not a Kodak moment!

I'll never forget that day ten years ago. Slacky rang on the Sunday to say that he'd managed forty stableford points in the individual event. How poignant. I'm still a nervous wreck thinking what it would have been like to fall into Moreton Bay from 15,000 feet. So he talks me through the sinking of a fifteen-foot putt for birdie on the eighteenth. Queenslanders are just so caring!

SUNDAY, 25 JANUARY 2004

THE WALKERVILLE LAWN TENNIS TITLE

It's the Sunday of the Australia Day long weekend. I'm in Adelaide to cover the one day international matches involving Australia and Zimbabwe.

I've deliberately kept myself tidy for today as I have a physical challenge ahead. This afternoon the Walkerville Tennis Open will be held at Jack and Sue Clarke's house in the leafy northern Adelaide suburb of Walkerville. Jack is a board member of Cricket Australia, a partner in a leading law firm and the best judge of wine in the whole of South Australia. His Australia Day Weekend barbecue has developed a reputation akin to the Tour de France— it is the survival of the fittest. His stately federation home boasts a lawn tennis court, and all the invited guests who fancy themselves at this ancient game have been invited to bring a racquet.

Some real power players of Australian cricket have been summoned: Bob Merriman and Creagh O'Connor will be there representing Cricket Australia; the big, gentle former West Indian great Clive 'Hubert' Lloyd, who oversaw the most vindictive period of concentrated fast bowling in West Indian cricket history, will attend; and a number of the Channel 9 commentary team will be there, notably Ian Healy, Mark Taylor and Simon O'Donnell.

I have no serious claims as a tennis player, but I had been having a regular practice hit with my son Daniel over the last few months and showing reasonable form on synthetic surfaces. The well-manicured grass of Walkerville will be different altogether.

I arrive at the Clarkes' at around two o'clock. Under my arm are my Bjorn Borg wooden racquet and two bottles of the most expensive red I could summon at a nearby liquor outlet. Jack greets me warmly at the door, takes my wine, inspects the brand and announces to Sue, 'Skull has bought some stuff that will go well in the cooking'. He's such a wine snob!

Ian Healy, despite some deft net touches, was a philosophical loser at tennis after being trounced by Simon O'Donnell

Other guests arrive in dribs and drabs. Some have bought a racquet, others will borrow from the Clarke collection.

There is no warm-up period when you attend a Jack Clarke barbecue. Two dozen bottles of his finest red have been opened and are airing close to where the sausages are sizzling. Guests are already strongly imbibing with unbridled enthusiasm. People are paddling up and down the pool and doing awful belly flops. And I'm drinking soda water—there is much to accomplish in just a while.

Jack bellows that the tennis should begin and initially it's just a few sets of friendly doubles. That suits me. I'm getting a good feel for the court surface. My forehand cross court is going well and will be a weapon at the business end of the day. Enough of the doubles, we need an overall singles winner, Jack announces. It is down to a field of four, me plus Healy the Queenslander, whose deft touches at the net appear to be his strength, but who is inconsistent and makes numerous unforced errors with his forehand; Taylor, who emerged from Wagga Wagga as an Australian Rules footballer and cricketer, but who on the evidence of his service action thinks a racquet is something that involves Al Capone; the dark horse, quite obviously, is the Victorian O'Donnell—strong and well coordinated, the former all-rounder came out of Assumption College, Kilmore, with a background in Australian Rules, cricket and whatever else he turned his hand to. 'Scoob' is going to be hard to beat. And there's me … a 'rallier' with a whippy cross-court forehand.

With just four entrants we're already at the semi-final stage, and at once Healy and O'Donnell are locked in battle. The Victorian's strength is built around his serve and volley game and he duly trounces the error-prone Healy 12–5. It has been decided to play every serve as a point, and the first to twelve with an advantage of two would go through to the final. Healy takes his loss philosophically and seeks consolation in a vat of the Barossa Valley's finest.

I'm up against Taylor. 'Tubby' could catch butterflies at first slip but his work on the grass with his big booming aluminium racquet leaves a lot to be desired. I'm waltzing him around the court, working him hard from left to right, and moreover I'm monstering his serve. In a short space of time I've recorded a 12–4 victory.

The final is up immediately. My opponent O'Donnell downs a beer—I decline. I'm ready for this big Victorian. The match gets underway without too much audience attention, although there is the odd chair that has been turned around to enjoy this classic battle between the younger O'Donnell and the wily leg-spinning veteran. O'Donnell's game is as expected, all about hustle and bustle, serving strongly and charging the net. To beat him I'll need my passing shots to work. The score has reached four. I'm making too many errors. His power game is threatening to crush me. I'm playing a lot of Lleyton Hewitt-type rallies—defending strongly but never hitting with a strength to pass the incredible wing span of the former St Kilda forward. At eight all it looks as if it's going to go to the wire, but suddenly there is a chink in the O'Donnell armour. His backhand, which has held up pretty well under his net challenges, has suddenly started to look a little ragged the more ground he is forced to cover. I start to direct all my shots to his backhand. Three times in a row he nets and the other he hits wide of the baseline. I lead 11–9. I need just one good serve. It's to the forehand court. He gets it back. I stay on

Simon O'Donnell displays some of his hitting power. He graciously accepted defeat at my hands at tennis, allowing me to be a crushing bore for two hours afterwards

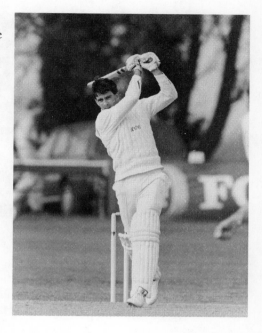

the baseline. I'm saying to myself, 'No errors here, Skull, the cup is yours with one O'Donnell error'. He's still in the point, the rally has gone for close to twenty shots. He pops one high back over the net. I should have smashed it away but decide to play the percentages and keep it in play. He lobs me. I chase back, turn, I need a clear winner. My forehand cross court just has to be the cup-winning stroke. It beats O'Donnell's lunge at the net, catches the line, and I've won 12–9. Simon is gracious in defeat and shakes my hand warmly at the net.

For the next two hours I am crushingly boring, talking about my triumph—how much I'd prepared and how badly I wanted to win—to anybody who'd listen. It means nothing to any of them. Nobody knew that I'd taken it this seriously. This was the ABC versus Channel 9—it was personal. I was defending 'Aunty'.

Clive Lloyd, the great West Indies captain, holds the winner's trophy after the ever- memorable inaugural World Cup at Lords', 1975

The food and the red are being consumed at a rapid rate. Guests are starting to fall like flies. I'm telling board chairman, Bob Merriman, what was wrong with cricket administration in the '70s—he's probably heard it all before. Clive Lloyd is seeking Jack's counsel, but doesn't seem to be understanding the host's rationale about Darren Lehmann's forthcoming hearing on a charge of racial abuse.

It's 2 am and the discussion is all about the wealthiest cricketers of our eras. I've volunteered Dennis Lillee. Healy says that he'll see my Lillee and raises me a Mark Taylor.

In a twinkling its 3 am and there's only Jack and me left. The barbecue has been turned off.

'Skull there's a bed inside for you if you'd like to kip the night,' the host kindly offers.

'I'll be there in a minute,' I volunteer. Then I begin a belated victory lap of the tennis court, the scene of my triumph some eleven hours earlier. Suddenly, I hit the net and trip. Getting up was going to be very difficult, so I grab a cushion off a nearby chair—it is to be my pillow for the night. I curl up just inside the backhand service box and sleep the sleep of a winner.

At 6 am I am awoken by water. It wasn't rain, it was Jack's sprinklers going off only a foot away from me. I think somebody is tipping a bucket of water over me. I am drenched. I have my wooden racquet, my dignity and nothing much else. I walk out onto the streets of Walkerville. A cab picks me up despite the state I'm in. I sit in the backseat and explain that I've slept on a sprinkler. Back at the hotel I get better sleep and rest till midday.

My ABC colleague, Jim Maxwell, knocks on the door, 'Are you ready to go to the ground?'.

I said, 'Damn straight,' although I'm far from ready. The commentary that afternoon is as good as I can manage in my state. I can barely see. Adjectives are kept to a minimum—the piece of cricket is either good or bad, nothing deeper than that. Apparently the professionalism at Channel 9 has also been compromised.

At sunset, Jack Clarke, my host from the night before, appears at the back of the box with an envelope for me. I'm in the commentary chair at the time going live to the country. Jack announces, 'Your room key, sir', and delivers the envelope. I open it. The contents are five blades of grass. Thank you, Jack. What a great host!

THE BEST TIME YOU CAN HAVE IN A CARPORT

After nearly a decade of contests this is to be the decider. There can be only one champion team in O'Keeffe Carport Cricket. I am ready. So are the other three. The pitch has not changed much during the ten years of competition—concrete rarely does!

We don't have a garage, we have a carport. It's roomy and accommodates two vehicles—in single file. We have lawn behind our house but there is a clothesline in the middle, so backyard cricket is out of the question. You know, the guy who designed clotheslines must have hated cricket. Hills Hoists have been one reason young Australians have occasionally taken to hanging round shopping malls instead of whiling away hours in brotherly cricket confrontations!

Over the years cricket at the O'Keeffes' has been all about the carport—and it has hosted some mighty battles. Between the ages of ten to sixteen my sons Daniel and Thomas were keen 'carport Pontings'. We played Test matches, and to make even sides of two Jonathon 'Jono' Gardner joined us. Jono is the same age as Daniel and they are great mates. They were one team and Tom, a year or so younger than the other boys, was my partner.

Our Tests were hard-fought affairs with plenty of pressure. The rules were simple. Each Test was a traditional four innings. The concrete pitch was just twelve yards long. Just short of a good length lay a grease patch. While the concrete surface was true and consistent, the same cannot be said about the grease patch. We played with a tennis ball, the less hair on it the better. There was no running between the wickets. Batsmen were either opening or at first drop—with two a side, you have no middle order or tail, which is good for the self-esteem, at the very least. Every time you hit the ball, you scored one run. Hit the ball past a rough line (seven yards in front of the stumps) and you had two. Strike it along the ground past the stumps line at the bowler's end for a boundary. Take a risk and strike it over that line on the full and you had six. The concrete wall at the back of the batting end of the carport was an automatic wicket-keeper. Snick it onto that slab of bricks on the full and you were out. Two garbage bins could be used as extra fielders—they were inevitably placed close on the off and on side respectively. You could bat forever. Lbw was a manner of dismissal but the batsman had to agree he was plumb or he got the benefit of the doubt. Strangely, there were very few disputes. For six years we must have had close to a hundred Test series. It was the happiest and most uncomplicated cricket I have ever played, anywhere!

Form guide on the combatants:

DANIEL O'KEEFFE: Genuine all-rounder. Capable of sharing the new tennis ball and batting in top two?! Very good outswing bowling action. Not a big spinner of the ball—it's a genetic thing, I'm told. Fine off side striker. Not strong off his legs. Clever reader of wrist spin—spots variations very quickly. Sound temperament. Excellent team man. Good judge of lbw—when he's bowling! Sure catcher—particularly off his own bowling.

JONO GARDNER: Promising soccer player—comes from a soccer-playing family. Wicket-keeper in underage cricket. Delivers medium pace 'nothing' balls. Tries the odd leg cutter. Always attempts to hit grease patch when bowling. Useful batsman. Tall and gets well forward. Can't pick my wrong 'un or flipper. I love bowling to Jono. Sorry, I digress. Very competitive. Shares a strong team ethic with Daniel. Can get nervous when batting close to a win. Reacts well to sledging. A thorough gentleman. Great bloke.

TOM O'KEEFFE: His favourite sports are swimming and surfing. Cricket appears too slow for him. Stiff, upright stance. Likes to hit the ball powerfully. Plays his shots from the outset. Hits across the line. In other words, a compulsive slogger. Handy pace bowler with slinging Jeff Thomson-like action. Possesses the sandshoe crusher. Sadly, has a very obvious slower ball—he keeps trying it, nonetheless, and I keep wearing the batsmen's inevitable bludgeoning swipe directly into the groin at shortish mid-on. Very single-minded. Resilient under pressure—has nerves of steel. An impact cricketer—when he's involved with bat or ball something seems to happen. Tom once admitted to me that he rarely blocked the ball because he didn't want to look a nerd!

KERRY O'KEEFFE: Well past his best. Still strokes the line of the ball religiously. Strictly adheres to the principle that any shot across the line is evil! Incapable of long innings because often takes risks by driving 'on the up' as physical condition and concentration deteriorate. Loves bowling—particularly to Jono. Wheels down his variations of leg spin, wrong 'uns and flippers with a variety of actions. Great mimic. Favours a version of the Richie Benaud side-on at release glide, but occasionally will embark on a spell of Abdul Qadirs, where his flailing arms and heavily spun googly do the Pakistani little justice. Valiantly tries to hit the grease patch with his flipper: lethal if it strikes oil; sits up and begs a boundary if it doesn't. Better with an old tennis ball—gets more pace off the deck with a hairless rock.

After five or so years of battle on the carport concrete, and with honours about even, it was unanimously decided by all four players that a Super Test be played to decide once and for all the champion team. Besides, the three teenagers had driver's licences and I sensed it was becoming less 'cool' to be seen playing cricket with a tennis ball and garbage bins.

Saturday, 5 November 2005 is to be the day. Late afternoon the match begins. Dan wins the toss and sends us in—my creaking 1978 Mercedes car had a particularly bad night and there is fresh oil on the grease patch.

Tom opens the batting. At once he is away, hitting regular straight fours and sixes. Dan always searches for the yorker against him, or tries to sneak one between bat and pad when bowling his off breaks. Tom might be stiff legged at the crease but he has the eye of a dead fish and the ball is finding the middle of his flashing blade. He is particularly savage on Jono because he is slower than Dan and more 'sloggable'. Having raced to a half-century he flashes at a quicker off break from Dan and edges to the automatic 'wicky' for a sparkling sixty-four.

I start slowly. A signature boringly mistake-free dig is required. This is a 150 plus pitch. Jono gets me to fizz off the grease patch and an lbw decision is debated. I reason that it is missing leg. Reluctantly Dan and Jono agree—it's sometimes good to have influence through age. I begin to strike regular fours as Dan

Dan O'Keeffe offers the full face as his brother Tom waits for a clean catch

drops short. By staying still and driving off the back foot down the line of the ball I am finding gaps between Jono at mid-on and Dan. Old-fashioned cricket works—ask Dizzy Gillespie after his double ton. At forty-four, I offer a simple caught and bowled and Jono snaffles it at the third attempt.

They're chasing a first innings total of 108 and are immediately in trouble. Tom yorks Dan and Jono is under pressure. I'm spinning it past his bat and the wrong 'uns keep going between a yawning bat and pad gap. He's reduced to a prodding shell of a batsman. Now for the flipper. It pitches, strikes grease, zoots and finds middle stump halfway up. On your bike, Jono! Jono and Dan have managed only twenty-two between them. Tom customarily suggests we should attack from the outset of our second innings and is lacing fours—four in succession off Jono before he tries once too often and is caught one-handed off the house wall.

Our lead is 110, I'm at the crease—and pumped! Neat forward defence shots for singles and the occasional thumping front foot off drive for four. Just like Dizzy. The lead is out to 145 when Dan gets one to bite and the bin at short leg takes me via the inside edge. They need 146 to be the all-time champions. Tom and I agree if we can get Dan early the pressure on Jono facing my leg breaks will be too much for the gentle kid from Kogarah Bay.

Dan is playing out of his fair skin, however. He's square cutting strongly—if you get it past the back steps where point would normally field, you get four. It's risky because any edge to the back wall is automatically out. Dan is pasting Tom's slower balls—they are tripe and I'm wearing them on the back and the legs at short mid-on. Within ten minutes, Dan has raised his bat for a century. It is customary to acknowledge a milestone in our game so Tom and I give him a generous round of applause. The reality confronting us is that Dan is going to chase down 146 by himself. The tennis ball's hair has gone shaggy and as a consequence there is no pace off the pitch. We're staring down the gun barrel. On 130, Dan makes a mistake: he tries to drive my dipping 'Richie Benaud' leg break and edges to slip. Yes! Still sixteen needed and Jono to bat under all sorts of pressure. He's very nervous—trying to let as many leg breaks go as he can—he's even letting wrong 'uns go but, to our frustration, they're bouncing over the top of middle stump. Tom is tired, he's bowled valiantly in stifling conditions. Jono somehow scrounges his way to ten. They now need six to win the Super Test. I begin a new over. I start with two leg breaks which beat a hesitant bat. You can cut the air with a knife. Tom is fairly phlegmatic but even he is groaning from mid-on at Jono's luck. Third ball just has to be the flipper. Jono would have known it's either going to be that skidder or a wrong 'un. I am at the top of my run-up. This is the ball which will determine the bragging rights for years to come. It pitches perfectly, right in the centre of the grease patch and it's shooting towards middle. Jono is at the top of his backlift, he's smelt a rat, he quickens his downstroke—and goes for glory. It's only a split second, I'm backing my flipper, but—crash—it's launched over Tom's head and is rising over my head and rising more! And out of the driveway, over the road it sails—high and handsome—finally coming to rest on the top of our neighbour Wim Smit's carport. A strike of fifty yards. Jono is the hero. Dan and he are high tenning. I can't believe it. I'm stunned. Tom heads to the kitchen for a Mars Bar—that kid gets over things very quickly. Dan and Jono are the champions.

That Jono straight drive haunts me every day as I reverse out of the drive because the tennis ball is still nestled squarely in the middle of Wim's carport roof. It will remain Jono Gardner's badge of honour forever. Great game, fellas!

There has not been another game of carport cricket since that day. Another chapter on fatherhood closes.

MY PUNTING SYSTEM ... A PROVEN WINNER AND LOSER

I've bumped into Trevor Marshallsea, a respected *Sydney Morning Herald* cricket writer, in a Sydney Airport lounge. Trevor writes skilfully and intelligently on the game yet has an air of somebody who would rather be doing something else. Despite appearances, he's a complete professional and is devoted to his trade. At the matches he covers Trevor can often be seen charging into a TAB outlet and you can be sure he emerges with a betting ticket loyal to his system.

One day during a quiet period at a Test match he explained his system to me. It revolves around horses improving with each start, so if a horse has finished seventh, fourth and third in its last three starts, Trevor is backing it to win that day. He seems to pull a lot of winners. I've been a punter myself for over forty years—and there is no romance about Australian horse racing. It's the pursuit of a quid that drives most of us. The most money I've ever won on a racehorse came courtesy of dear old Vivatus, a gelding I part owned in the early '80s. Vivatus enabled me to stave off a regular job for a couple of years.

Like most punters I've yearned for that elusive successful system. You know, a formula that spits out regular winners at the racetrack and guarantees a return if rigidly adhered to. Richie Benaud has a system. He calculates the most likely winner of a horserace by a series of equations involving jockey rating, weight, recent form and barrier draw. Richie swears by it. I've travelled with him on a Friday where he will sit in seat 1A of a Qantas jet and execute his strategies for the next day's meeting using the data in *Sportsman* and *Timeform*. I have also returned to Sydney on a Sunday where he will sit in 1A again and review how his system has gone by devouring the results in the racing section of

Richie Benaud, here with fellow Channel 9 cricket commentator Tony Grieg, has a punting system, but I've never seen any evidence that the great man actually uses it!

the newspaper. He seems to jag lots of winners. I've never really seen any evidence that the Channel 9 cricket front man actually punts his system. It would appear that Richie 'paper trades' brilliantly. But so do thousands, I reckon.

The real proof of a genuine betting system is how it actually goes in the heat of battle. When your hard earned is in a bookmaker's pocket for the duration of a race—and there is the very real prospect that it will stay there forever. I'm not saying Richie doesn't have the 'bottle' for it, but it's a false reputation to have a winning system and not trade it. Maybe the great man can punt it in his eighties instead of either playing lawn bowls or, more likely, still hosting television cricket coverage.

I have a system, myself—or to be more precise, I pinched it off somebody else! In the mid '80s I used to hang around racetracks: desperate, broke, hopeless!

On a wet and miserable Wyong Wednesday I was in the public bar at the racecourse and feeling flatter than a Shaun Tait sandshoe crusher. I was drinking multiple schooners of Tooheys New with 'Jukesy' (Tom Jukes). Both of us had backed five consecutive losers. Jukesy is a good bloke, a former Newcastle wharfie I played 'bat ball' with at Bar Beach Surf Club—we also consumed the Red Sea in schooners of ale. Jukesy and I used to hang out a lot with the late Brian Carlson, a rugby league legend, when I spent a couple of years living in Newcastle. This was not a particularly sober period of my life.

Back to Wyong. Race six was won by a rough-headed gelding which had run some sort of race on the previous Saturday at Broadmeadow. Neither Jukesy nor I was on it.

'That horse is a Downsey, you know,' he mumbled.

'What's a Downsey?' I asked out of respect.

'It's a horse which qualifies for a particular system by having raced in the last ten days and its last two finishes add up to eight or less—a bloke named Downes invented it and it works sometimes,' he ventured.

Sometimes, eh! Well, given that I have zero wins from five wagers, sometimes is good, really good. I was interested in anything to stem the bleeding from my pocket, but Jukesy didn't know too much more about it.

I then bumped into Larry Hawke, a knockabout bookmaker who gave the system a wrap! 'Yeah, it's the invention of Frank Downes, a stonemason from the Sutherland Shire, and some people swear by it,' opined Larry.

From that day I decided to follow it and keep records. I figured it would return more than the collective specials of Ian Craig, Rod Gallegos and Paul Ambrosoli. The system, as I shaped it, goes like this: add up the last two placings of a horse. If they total eight or less and the horse has had a race start in the last ten days, it is a pre-qualifier. Then I decided, after trialling it in this form for a month or so, that the odds of the horse had to be between 2–1 and 7–1 and the wager an each-way transaction.

For over twelve months I paper traded the system on Sydney, Melbourne, Brisbane and Adelaide Saturday and mid-week race meetings. My records were religiously detailed, the profit or loss tabled and the trends noted. After a year and a half it was obvious that the system worked best on certain race courses. Please find my seeded list below:

1 Sandown

2 Warwick Farm

3 Randwick

4 Flemington

5 Caulfield

6 Rosehill

7 Eagle Farm

8 Canterbury

9 Moonee Valley

10 Doomben

11 Cheltenham

12 Morphettville.

Sandown and Warwick Farm were the standouts. The winning returns on these two tracks were virtually guaranteed, particularly on rain-affected days in winter. Randwick was ranked third and Flemington fourth—both showed better than average profit but, sadly, it fell away after this quartet. Doomben and the two Adelaide courses were fair dinkum bookmaker donation organisations. I decided to live off Sandown and Warwick Farm. Say goodbye to poverty, Kessy, this system is foolproof.

There were words of caution however. Leviathan bookmaker Colin Tidy told me one day that he would take on any system punter, anywhere, anytime. 'System Sam hung himself' is a chestnut in the industry. Well, I'm no Sam.

Anyway I started well. Within two months I had built a bank of $2000 into $10,000, betting $100 each way on all qualifiers between the odds of 2–1 and 7–1.

In the early '90s I was invited to pay in a Golden Oldie cricket match in Darwin. The match was scheduled for a Sunday and they were racing on a heavy ground at Sandown on the Saturday. Perfect!

I flew to Darwin with my $10,000 bank. It was time to win some serious dough. There were five qualifiers at that Sandown meeting. All were going to be within the odds of the system. I was going in for the kill. I decided to lift my wagering to $1000 each way on each qualifier.

I'm at Fannie Bay Racetrack in Darwin, but I'm not interested in the locals, I'm punting Sandown! The Darwin bookmakers fielding on the interstate meetings are only too willing to accommodate this blow-in from the south-east.

I'm drinking with former left-arm orthodox tweaker Ray Bright and trying to explain how my system is a sure thing and

Ray Bright during his left-arm orthodox tweaker days. He also tweaked a few winners while I went down by $10,000!

how it is going to be my superannuation scheme. The Victorian looks less than impressed but is shouting in turn and darting out for a $5.00 each way wager every twenty minutes.

The Sandown meeting has begun and in race two my chosen steed runs fifth—minus $2000! In the third, the system nag runs eighth—minus $4000! Not to worry, the qualifier in race five is 6–1 and a noted mudlark. I'll get out of this hole. The chosen thoroughbred shapes to win just before the turn then falls—minus $6000! Things are now tragic. 'Brighty' has just won $32.00 on a Darwin race. I'm happy for him. No, I'm not, I'm shitty. He's grinning like a Wiggle and I'm $6000 down.

Systems work because you are a machine and you stick to them religiously. I'm committed to bet on the next two qualifiers, the law of averages is behind me. My $2000 on the race six qualifier is duly placed in the hands of the leading Darwin bookie. I don't think he even laid off! It ran a tired second last and I'm minus $8000.

Brighty's backed a 20–1 third at Doomben. On ya, Ray!

I'm now very nervous. The final race at Sandown pops out a 13–2 shot. I can get out of this—the system has never, in almost two years, had a day where there is not even a placed hope. On goes the $1000 each way. Brighty shouts a round. He's having a good day—he's up $39.00. Great!

As I place the final bet my bookie offers to fly me to Darwin from Sydney every week if I'd punt exclusively with him. Smart arse! They're off in the last. My horse is sixth at the 600, fourth at the 400, second at the 200. Go you good thing! Shit, it's weakening. Oh no, hang on, hang on! No! Beaten by an eyelash for a gallant fourth! Minus $10,000! It's over.

Brighty shouts a roady at the member's bar. And then we're at Darwin Golf Club for a function. All the boys are pissed after an enjoyable eighteen holes of golf.

'How was your day, Skull?' asks Greg Chappell innocently.

The answer and the rest of the night is a blur.

I've rarely punted the system seriously again! Every time I see a meeting at Sandown, however, I'm tempted—and okay I have backed system horses at that venue in recent times. I'm going to have another day where I punt my strategy at Sandown on a heavy track. Marshallsea can have his improved placings formula, but give me the Downsey any day—except if I'm at Fannie Bay!

SUNDAY, 12 MARCH 2006

THE NEW WORLD
ONE DAY RECORD

I'm enjoying my role as tour leader of an Australian supporters' group in South Africa. There are 127 enthusiasts in my party and although we've been together for only nine days, some firm friendships have already formed. And there is no shortage of characters.

My evenings are spent in the company of a larger-than-life fella named Andrew 'Doylie' Doyle. Doylie's favoured tipple is Scotch. He drinks beer but he argues that spirits keep his weight manageable at 147 kilograms! Doylie has done reasonably well in real estate around Alice Springs and is a committee man on the Northern Territory Cricket Board. He has a sharp mind but is less focused in regard to responsible drinking.

A regular in our drinking group is Barry 'Baz' Young, a charismatic former Gyprock tradesman from Mildura. Cigarettes have robbed Baz of his voice box and in its place is a large hole at the top of his oesophagus. When he is straining to make a point late at night, that volcanic crater can spit an amount of phlegm that would adequately irrigate inland Australia.

Wilbur, a quietly spoken storeman from Adelaide, occasionally joins our shout. He prefers to sit out among the South African crowd on match day and has frequently returned to base a little wounded. Castle lager is the beer of choice for most Afrikaners. It's a very nice drop, too—and because it contains precious little preservatives our party has agreed that you can drink a small lake of it and wake up feeling okay the next day. That's the overview anyway—and Wilbur is a strong Castle disciple.

My tour, thus far, has been eventful. At Port Elizabeth I ventured alone to Pollok Beach on the Summerstrand coast close to sunset to surf the warm waves of the Indian Ocean. After an hour of most enjoyable body surfing it was time to shower. As I made my way to the shower/toilet block near the surf club car park, I was followed by a middle-aged male in T-shirt and shorts. I needed to use the urinal but just as I was to enter the male toilet my new best friend approached and asked if he could help me in any way. Suddenly I lost my urge to pee, to shower, to hang around for that matter. I bolted 300 metres back to our hotel. I was shocked—and I'm from Sydney!

Less stressful have been the three days spent at the Hluhluwe Game Reserve near Durban, where late-evening game drives were followed by a traditional braai featuring delicious boerewors sausages—I managed to scoff five of them at one gluttonous sitting. Nobody has ever lost weight hosting cricket tours.

Today we're in Johannesburg for the fifth and final one day international between Ricky Ponting's men and the South Africans.

Adam Gilchrist looks on as Graeme Smith, the South African captain, survives a stumping

With the series level at 2–2, Australia has been stretched by Graeme Smith's squad but has impressive form at the Wanderers Stadium—having won a World Cup final there in 2003—and is a well-fancied favourite. Ponting calls correctly and soon after Adam Gilchrist and Simon Katich are pinning their ears back. This Wanderers pitch is a bowler's nightmare. Any dot ball is roundly applauded. The Proteas' fast medium bowler Roger Telemachus manages to deliver a maiden over and the home crowd gives him a worshipping ovation more often associated with the Dalai Llama.

Gilchrist (55) is the first to fall in the sixteenth over with the score at ninety-seven. The new man, Ponting, does a Russell Crowe and, on his own command, unleashes hell! Rarely has the captain struck them more cleanly. Balls are disappearing into the crowd over cover and long-off when he's civil and deep mid wicket when he decides to be crude.

Katich (seventy-nine from ninety balls), by comparison, is as slow moving as a Bert Newton game show. The New South Wales left-hander's value is undeniable but his problem appears in others' perception of him.

Mike 'Mr Cricket' Hussey has come in and employs his power game. Stuff icing any cake, he's going to be a sizeable chunk of the pastry today. Mr Cricket clubs eighty-one off fifty-one balls with nine boundaries and three sixes. Still, it is Ponting, with a one-day career best of 164 from 105 balls faced, who sees Australia establish a new one day international record total of 434 from fifty overs.

Seamer Johan van der Wath with 0–76 from ten overs is the tightest bowler. That's a little like winning *Big Brother* and not being a complete tool!

The Wanderers Stadium boasts the most vocal section of

Mike 'Mr Cricket'' Hussey plays a delicate shot during his powerful innings

spectators in world cricket. It is an area known as the 'bullring', but today it was the 'library'! Australian supporters aside, the terraces were generally deathly quiet as sixes and fours resonated off the visitors' blades.

Between innings, I'm in the media area for lunch and one South African journalist is salivating over his potential review of Smith and his team. 'I'll be calling for at least six sackings—and the head of the skipper,' he announces.

Information reaches me via the Proteas that two quirky comments in the South African dressing-room before the run chase began may just have been the catalyst for the unbelievable outcome that occurred in three hours' time. The first came from all-rounder Andrew Hall (1–80 from ten overs), who, while sitting with his team-mates, bowed his head in silence for ten minutes, then slowly rose and observed, 'Right boys, the bowlers have done their job. Now it's up to the batters.' Apparently the whole room erupted in laughter before a degree of introspection returned, only to be broken a short time later by the sight of Jacques Kallis, a man of few words normally, getting to his feet, staring at his team-mates and announcing, 'I reckon they're a dozen short!' Again screams of mirth rang around the shed as the opening batsmen padded up. These sorts of tongue-in-cheek comments can be watershed moments when sports teams are faced with Herculean tasks.

The South African start is uglier than Mrs Doubtfire. Boeta Dippenaar (1) edges Nathan Bracken into his stumps in the second over and at 1–3, needing 435 to win, the locals prospects look as forlorn as the chances of John Howard inviting Peter Costello over for a sausage sizzle and a belly full of piss. And talking of sinking a few, the number three batsman is Herschelle

Herschelle Gibbs never played better—seven prodigious sixes in his 175

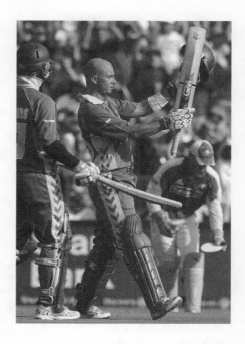

Gibbs—a shaven-headed smarty pants (in Australian eyes, anyway)—who allegedly was sighted on the drink at a Jo'burg nightclub at 2 am that morning. A run rate required of 11.44 with a hangover is not everybody's cup of lager!

Gibbs and Smith meet in the middle and decide not to panic. Wait for the four ball and re-assess in a few overs. Well, the four balls come and come, so do the bloody six balls. And the next wicket falls at 190. Smith is out for ninety from just fifty-five deliveries. Gibbs's bat looks bionic. He's never played better.

Victoria's reverse swing man Mickey Lewis is racing to his own personal career best (0–113 from ten overs).

I'm sitting near Neil and Mary Holton from Woodville Cricket Club in Adelaide—they're terrific cricket people but are hard-pressed to enjoy the carnage being reeked upon our national bowling line-up. And the home crowd is not helping. Every time a boundary is struck they're turning to us in the stands and singing 'Aussie, Aussie, Aussie. Baa! Baa! Baa!'. Apparently we are confused with New Zealanders over here—if they want to sledge us they tend to intimate to a man that we have all had sexual relations with sheep, that as pubescent teenagers we've taken lambs up to Brokeback Mountain and all that baloney.

Still, Gibbs is finally out for 175 (twenty-one boundaries and seven prodigious sixes) and Kallis makes a cameo appearance. But Mark Boucher is annoying us again. Sorry to be a touch biased, but two paralytic Afrikaners sitting behind me have just about worn out their welcome with their constant harping and occasional spilling of a Castle lager down my back. Boucher is squirting boundaries through impossible gaps and the target is now very gettable.

I needed something stronger than lager after the Proteas won with a ball to spare

Numbers nine and ten, Telemachus and Hall, come and go. And with three balls of the final over remaining, they still need two to win. If Brett 'Bing' Lee can rissole Makhaya Ntini first ball, I'm going to turn around to Johann and Os and give them the biggest raspberry this fifty-seven-year-old can muster. Stuff it. Ntini's angled one to third man and Boucher has the strike.

The scores are level. I'll still give the Boers the bird if it's a tie. Crap! Boucher's belted 'Bing' for a boundary and I'm buckling. World record! The crowd goes nuts. The Baa Baas intensify. I'm off to the bar. Where's Doylie? I don't drink Scotch but I need something stronger than Castle lager. What goes on while on tour, stays on tour. The rest of that night shall remain that way.

South Africa v. Australia
Australia in South Africa 2005–06 (5th ODI)

Australia innings		Runs	Balls	Mins	4s	6s
+AC Gilchrist	c Hall b Telemachus	55	44	68	9	–
SM Katich	c Telemachus b Ntini	79	90	134	9	1
*RT Ponting	c Dippenaar b Telemachus	164	105	153	13	9
MEK Hussey	c Ntini b Hall	81	51	75	9	3
A Symonds	not out	27	13	22	3	1
B Lee	not out	9	7	11	–	–
DR Martyn	did not bat					
MJ Clarke	did not bat					
NW Bracken	did not bat					
SR Clark	did not bat					
ML Lewis	did not bat					
Extras (4 lb, 10 nb, 5 w)		19				
Total (4 wickets, innings closed, 50 overs)		434				

Fall of wickets: 1–97 (Gilchrist, 15.2 ov), 2–216 (Katich, 30.3 ov), 3–374 (Hussey, 46.1 ov), 4–407 (Ponting, 47.4 ov)

South Africa bowling	Overs	Mdns	Runs	Wkts	Wides	No-Balls
Ntini	9	0	80	1	1	–
Hall	10	0	80	1	–	2
van der Wath	10	0	76	0	1	1
Telemachus	10	1	87	2	3	7
Smith	4	0	29	0	–	–
Kallis	6	0	70	0	–	–
Kemp	1	0	8	0	–	–

South Africa innings		Runs	Balls	Mins	4s	6s
*GC Smith	c Hussey b Clarke	90	55	100	13	2
HH Dippenaar	b Bracken	1	7	6	–	–
HH Gibbs	c Lee b Symonds	175	111	142	21	7
AB de Villiers	c Clarke b Bracken	14	20	43	1	–
JH Kallis	c and b Symonds	20	21	22	1	–
+MV Boucher	not out	50	43	77	4	–
JM Kemp	c Martyn b Bracken	13	17	20	–	–
JJ van der Wath	c Ponting b Bracken	35	18	20	1	3
R Telemachus	c Hussey b Bracken	12	6	10	2	–
AJ Hall	c Clarke b Lee	7	4	8	1	–
M Ntini	not out	1	1	4	–	–
Extras	(4 b, 8 lb, 4 nb, 4 w)	20				
Total	(9 wickets, 49.5 overs)	438				

Fall of wickets: 1–3 (Dippenaar, 1.2 ov), 2–190 (Smith, 22.1 ov), 3–284 (de Villiers, 30.5 ov), 4–299 (Gibbs, 31.5 ov), 5–327 (Kallis, 37.4 ov), 6–355 (Kemp, 42.1 ov), 7–399 (van der Wath, 46.3 ov), 8–423 (Telemachus, 48.2 ov), 9–433 (Hall, 49.3 ov)

Australia bowling	Overs	Mdns	Runs	Wkts	Wides	No-Balls
Lee	7.5	0	68	1	1	3
Bracken	10	0	67	5	–	–
Clark	6	0	54	0	–	–
Lewis	10	0	113	0	1	1
Symonds	9	0	75	2	–	–
Clarke	7	0	49	1	–	–

Source: Courtesy of cricketarchive.com

SKULLA CROWNIE'S MAIDEN VICTORY

Two months shy of twenty-five years ago, I part-owned a thoroughbred horse that won a nondescript mid-week distance race at Royal Randwick. It was one of the great thrills of my sporting life—and was more than just a little financially rewarding when you consider the noble beast's starting price of 125–1! That champion's name was Vivatus and despite the fact that post-race discussions surrounded the winning of the Melbourne Cup that year, this was to be the brave gelding's last victory. Retirement, in fact, was just weeks away.

A quarter of a century later I have my next chance to own a winner. This time the venue, unfortunately, is not Randwick but, indeed, Narromine—a respectable farming town in central western New South Wales which has produced notable sportsmen like David Gillespie, Glenn McGrath and Melinda Gainsford-Taylor.

I am a one-tenth shareholder in a gallant steed called Skulla Crownie. Today he will represent ten people in race three on the Narromine card. All nine of the other part-owners are country folk from around the Dubbo area. There are more pairs of moleskin trousers in their wardrobes than there have been moronic *Big Brother* evictees. My great friend and Narromine businessman David 'Ringers' Ringland chose Skulla at the Scone yearling sales a year or so ago. He rang me enthusiastically after the purchase to declare that we would be racing a well-conformed son of the successful American stallion Beautiful Crown. He sounded very bullish about its prospects. David then formed the syndicate which included Robert and Nerida Atkinson—who found success as sole owners of that lucky crab?? and Stradbroke Handicap winner, Sniper's Bullet. Excuse my resentment, but I wish we'd bought Sniper's Bullet—that, however, is another story. I should move on. Also among the owners are the likeable Dubbo accountant John Ferrari and one of the central west's best known larrikins, Allan Marks. We're a happy group, and we'll be a lot merrier this afternoon if Skulla Crownie can be first to salute the judge.

It is the two-year-old's second race start. I'd made the three-hour drive from Sydney to Mudgee for his less-than-auspicious debut in January. It was a 1000-metre maiden and our boy ran a tiring eighth out of nine—and pulled up shin sore. Still, Bradman batted number seven on Test debut and failed.

Our trainer, Tracey Bartley—a former jockey who has established a strong reputation as a horseman—is more confident today. Skulla has been working 'the place down' and hopes are high for a forward showing. The accomplished jockey Matthew

Cahill has the booking and Skulla has drawn well in barrier five in a twelve-horse field.

We're not expecting generous odds from the bookmakers—the Narromine satchel swingers are notoriously tighter than a McGrath maiden over—and the best we can get is 3–1. The tote is offering $4.40 for the win. That's where we do most of the wagering. Bartley and Cahill both feel that Skulla has a huge chance in this field and everybody has put their money down. Skulla is placed in the barrier early and, although one or two of his opponents are playing up, his manners would make Richie Benaud look uncouth.

The gates fly open and Cahill jumps him perfectly. He positions Skulla just off the leader's neck and on the bit. At 400 metres, Ringers—normally an understated individual—leaps onto the lawn and starts screaming his support. Around the turn Skulla draws level with the leader, then kicks a length clear. Can he hold on?? Can he what! At the post, his winning margin is 1.8 lengths—and reasonably hard held, at that. There is an irregular amount of embracing and kissing among the owners. Males kiss males when your horse wins its maiden— it's a racecourse thing—I can't explain it. We've all got money. And we have an above-average galloper. Naturally, all the post-race chat is about qualifying for the Golden Slipper. It's every owner's right to get carried away. Sure, this was a modest maiden in flyblown Narromine, but you've got to shoot for the stars.

Ringers keeps telling anyone who cares to listen that it is his eye for a horse which has resulted in our good fortune. His charming wife, Heather, tempers every boast with 'Oh David, please'—rural women are so realistic. This, however, was no time for reality. This was beer o'clock—and the ale flowed.

After a while at the Narromine races everybody looks like Glenn McGrath, and there are any number of his relatives around the place. If you've had a few beers, a good rule of thumb if you can't remember someone's name is to just call him Macca and you'll be close!

Skulla Crownie has broken his duck in only his second start—perhaps the Slipper might be a little rich, but we're going to have a lot of fun around the bush racetracks with this fella. Twenty-five years between winners is a fair drought, but this day was worth waiting for!

THE CRICKET LADDER— THE JOURNEY UP ISN'T THAT EASY!

The cricket season is up and running. District cricket has been going now for almost a month and the first-class program has begun. I'm watching Campbelltown play St George in a fourth-grade match at Harold Fraser Park. I've come to watch the son of a friend of mine, one Adam Coyte—seen by many as the most promising fifteen-year-old all-rounder in the state. His father, Peter, a former lower grader for Penrith, has sired a number of gifted cricketers already, notably his daughter Sarah, who continues to dominate women's cricket each weekend around Sydney. Young Adam has come in with his team needing only a handful of runs for victory, but his stroke play in scoring fifteen not out reminded me of David Hookes. The ball is spearing off this left-hander's blade. The whip through mid wicket, the full-blooded slap through extra cover—this kid's got something. I have a brief chat to his father afterwards and we both agree how tough the climb to the top will be for any promising youngster. Hell, I reckon it's the toughest of all sporting climbs!

You start out as a gifted, naive teenager graded in your District fourth XI. Every summer Saturday afternoon you seem to be at some godforsaken outer suburban oval where flies carry you out to bat in forty-degree temperatures. While your mates are getting up to all sorts of shenanigans with chicks from the local surf club, you're asking for 'middle stump' guard from an octogenarian with Coke-bottle glasses and a hearing aid. He gives you an approximate! Your only female company is a 120-kilogram scorer who has already demolished her second packet of chocolate biscuits and is eagerly waiting to record your dismissal because full of piss you sledged her the previous Saturday night. You have only just arrived at the crease and your opponents are abusing you for being a 'big-headed poofter'!

In time your performances in the lower grade justify selection in first grade—where snarling thirty-five year olds give you multiple 'send-offs' when they con the nervous wreck of an umpire to win dodgy lbw decisions in their favour, and each time you show any emotion as you pass by their outside edge with the ball you are told in no uncertain terms to just 'Get back to your mark and bowl son'!

If you're lucky you get to the next level: first-class cricket. Suddenly your every failure is recorded in the national newspapers. You're subjected to turning up to start the obligatory warm-up before the sun has risen. Almost at once you get news of your sacking from the team because of inconsistency and brashness. It is delivered by a pissed-up journalist who tries to get you to slag the selectors.

If you survive all this, you're in the Test team. You get to hang around with Warney, send lewd text messages, binge drink, and learn to duck king hits from 150-kilogram juiced-up muscle-laden bouncers. Eventually the tabloid newspapers call for your dropping. You respond with a career-saving century and immediately give the finger to the press box on national television. You are fined half your match fee, dropped anyway for disciplinary reasons, and the Chairman of Selectors says you're not being dropped just rotated for at least six years. You retire abruptly, seek a job in the media, get frustrated and eventually accept the role of computer analyst for the Nepal national team, where you convert to Buddhism and bore everybody to death on your return to Australia.

A tough ladder to climb, you'd agree, but better than a real job!

HOW I BECAME A SINGLE-FIGURE GOLFER

I've awoken from a good sleep. I'm booked for eighteen holes of golf at the prestigious Lakes Golf Club at Kensington. I'm in love with this wonderful game.

My host is Tony O'Rourke, a single-figure marker who has aspirations to be the club president. Tony is a St Joseph's College old boy, who made few tackles in the school's sixth-grade rugby team, but who can play the piano like Liberace. He is tremendous company on the golf course with a quirky sense of humour and a wonderful turn of phrase.

Over the last thirty-odd years I've dabbled in golf. I've gone through the addiction phase—it lasted a couple of months—but I'm over it. I now only get up at 3 am two or three times a week to practise putting in my office after visiting the bathroom. Nude putting in the dead of night gives a tremendous psychological edge. I mean, who else in this country at that time is practising sinking eight footers? Nobody except me!

I never took golf seriously—that is until three years ago. I once heard John Singleton say that the progression to the grave is golf, lawn bowls, death, and that he refused to embark on the first part of that downward spiral. 'Singo' hated golf with a passion. Still does. But I believe that if I stay at golf for a few decades I can bypass lawn bowls and exit gracefully at ninety while clearing a lob wedge prior to eighteen holes at The Australian. There could be worse ways to go. (As you may have detected, I'm only mildly addicted.)

So in 2003 I made the decision that golf was to be my sport for the next twenty-five years or so. I joined Bexley Golf Club, a rather short course in the southern suburbs of Sydney, with a par of a mere sixty-two and not a single par five hole. Some regard Bexley as easier than Paris Hilton. My official handicap after handing in the obligatory cards, was set at eighteen. In stableford events I would be getting a stroke every hole. In other words, every par I managed was worth three points. My journey had begun—my goal was to whittle my handicap to every weak golfers Shangri-la—single figures! For that to happen, however, I needed assistance. My swing was shit. I couldn't chip and my putting stroke would have made Diego Maradona look balanced. Paul Davis, the Bexley professional, became my friend and mentor. His advice was always considerate and timely. Paul and I played countless mid-week competition rounds together where he would only give me pointers at the nineteenth. My handicap began to shrink: sixteen, fourteen, twelve (for three frustrating months), ten and then, finally, after thirty-nine points on a hot

November Saturday stableford event, I was off nine. Single figures! Little old me!

The following Saturday, my first as a genuine A grader, gave some the impression that I had become a little too pleased with myself. Was it the swagger, the Tiger Woods body-hugging T-shirt. Or was it more that I suggested—after a few schooners in the club house—that it would be nice if Bexley had an exclusive single-figure bar? A place where we low markers could drink among our own. Where fifteen markers could dream of one day sharing an ale with us single-digit men. Where the talk would be of birdies and the senior circuit rather than pondering about joining the local lawn bowling club. Okay, my colleagues didn't warm to the idea—initially—or even after a few more beers. In fact, to be frank, they turned on me! I was derided—told to get a life, and booed into the cab. Fickle! Sensitive! Fair dinkum, it was only a suggestion.

Since that day my game has ebbed and flowed. The lowest I've been is seven. I am now off nine. Thoughts of a single-figure bar are long gone. I'm determined, however, to get to a handicap of six and be able to front for every game of golf knowing that I'm a better than even money chance of playing to it. I need to improve my chipping and putting, which will mean long hours down at the Scarborough Park back field, aiming at a stump from twenty metres. It's deja vu! Scarborough Park, Kogarah, is where I bowled endlessly at a stump to hone my spinning talents. It is where my modest ability at golf has been developed as well. There are always rumours that it will in the near future become a motorway. Hell! If it does, I'll be back in creams, aiming at a jack with a large black ball, drinking nips of Scotch—and be one step closer to the grave. No motorway please, Mr Premier!

It's almost tee off time at the Lakes. A microphone crackles and Dave, the amiable Englishman in the starters' cubicle, announces the next group to make their way to the first tee. 'The Lakes would like to welcome the group of Mr Tony O'Rourke, Mr Albert Salerno and their guests Mr Jim Taylor from Terrey Hills and Mr Kerry O'Keeffe from the Royal Bexley Country Club.'

Everybody on the practice putting green cracks up laughing as I sheepishly make my way to the tee off zone. Golf is so elitist.

Four hours later we're back in the club house. O'Rourke had a blinding day and will undoubtedly win the A-grade competition with forty-two points. Albert's short game stood him in good stead and he played to his handicap of seven. Jim had a nightmare and is drinking furiously in an effort to seek refuge. I scrambled to return thirty-three points. Not quite playing to my handicap but once the wind comes up at the Lakes, your iron play has to be so precise. Mine still needs work. Tony suggests I should join the club. It's only $33,000 initial payment he emphasises. My jaw drops. That's a deposit on a harbour-side apartment! A round at Bexley for $15.00 has never looked so attractive.

SUNDAY, 12 NOVEMBER 2006

SKULL—
THE NICKNAME

I'm driving my son Tom to Elouera Beach, just north of Cronulla, for his surf training session. We've pulled up at traffic lights on Taren Point Road. A late model Holden stops slowly beside us. A teenager winds down the passenger seat window, offers his thumb out the window and quite politely says, 'Hi Skull', and winds the window back up. The occupants of the car all fall about laughing, but it was a friendly gesture, one that I'm used to these days; I appreciate that people get a kick out of addressing me by my nickname.

'Skull' has been my moniker for over forty years. I'm quite fond of it. It's not that it's like 'Mad Dog' or 'Schooners' or 'Sloth'. And it's so much better than KOK. I reckon initials as a nickname are a cop out—it suggests that people are struggling to find some love or even a weakness in you. Some felt that, given my first book, *According to Skull,* was something of an autobiography,

I should have explained the history of 'Skull' somewhere. Well, I'm correcting that oversight.

As with many nicknames, it originated from an innocent aside in a cricket dressing-room in 1965. At that time professional wrestling was all the rage in Australia. A Sydney promoter, Jim Barrett, had brought over a number of huge Americans to strut their stuff for Aussie audiences. Along with thousands, I loved it. My favourite was Skull Murphy, a bald Canadian who scared everybody with his manic personality and roughhouse tactics.

One wet afternoon—while playing third-grade District cricket for St George as a fifteen-year-old at Cahill Park, Tempe—I was involved in some impromptu wrestling in the change rooms. I had just had my hair cut very short (Skull Murphy was bald after all), and declared that I was the Skull and I'd beat anybody with my favourite move—the Power Slam. As I recall, I lost every bout that day! Anyway, Peter Auliffe, our whimsical opening bowler who dealt in outswingers and witty asides, christened me 'Skull'—despite my tragic win–loss record. And forty-one years later, I'm still called Skull.

The real Skull Murphy died in 1970, aged thirty-nine, after overdosing on sleeping pills. His best moments in the ring came when he partnered the dreaded Brute Bernard to win a number of tag-team belts. Brute was also as bald as a billiard ball and, ironically, also died young of a self-inflicted gunshot wound. Steve Bernard, the longstanding Australian cricket team manager, was a team-mate of mine in the '70s. The moment he emerged as a wild fast bowler from Orange in regional New South Wales he was known as 'Brute'. That wrestling era has much to answer for in terms of cricketing nicknames.

I've decided to shave my head as a Skull Murphy legacy—apparently Skull was meticulous that not a single hair appeared on his body. Thank you, Skull, this shave's for you!

THE ASHES—THEY MEAN A LOT!

It's early morning and I'm walking the dogs in Carss Park, which is the most pleasant of strolls. Kogarah Bay is as calm as a mill pond. The sun is shining, fellow walkers are saying 'Good morning' as they pass. Life is good. The only downside is the smell of chlorine from Dick Caine's nearby swimming pool complex. It's a little overpowering at this time of the morning.

My thoughts are being concentrated by an interview conducted on air with the always interesting Geoff 'Henry' Lawson. Henry's talking about the pleasure and satisfaction he got from victory over England; how consuming it was to play against the old enemy when he first emerged from Wagga Wagga in the late '70s as a bespectacled teenager with a prodigious talent to bowl fast. His story is typical of many over the years.

From the moment an Australian child picks up a bat and ball he is given two cricket tips—don't walk and don't lose to the

Geoff Lawson is mugged after taking a wicket at Old Trafford 1989. Geoff got great satisfaction from victory over the Old Enemy

Poms! I became a walker and lost to England—it's something I've had to live with for forty-odd years.

The Ashes series was the real deal. Very little else seemed to matter. My only memories of the Ashes as a boy are of waking up at 2 am with the transistor earpiece around my face and Len Coldwell, the English seamer, bowling. Len Coldwell was always bowling. His run-up must have woken me up twenty times that Australian winter in the early 1960s. I don't know if dear old Len was any good but he could certainly stir me from a deep sleep. And he could sleep himself, apparently. Blessed with an English midlander's milk-white skin, Len fell asleep while sun baking on Bondi Beach one hot afternoon during the 1963 MCC tour and had to be taken to hospital suffering first-degree burns! Lenny was a fast bowler, after all! Spinners go to tanning centres!

When I was growing up, somehow I came to believe that the polite English knew the game inside out and that it was nice of them to let us convicts play against them occasionally. Even when I walked out to bat in my debut Test match at the Melbourne Cricket Ground, that nice chap, the late Sir Colin Cowdrey, offered, 'All the best, young man, but not too much luck'.

How smashing! The Poms even wish you well when they play you. But then John Snow snapped me back to reality by hitting me in the chest with a vicious bumper and spewing, 'Take that, faggot!' Still, as I writhed on the ground, convinced my heart had been terminally damaged, Sir Col saved the day with, 'Are you alright, young 'un?'. Stuff Snow, Col's me mate!

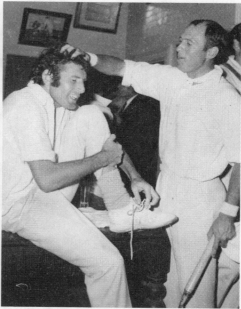

When nasty John Snow landed a bumper on my chest, the late Sir Colin Cowdrey (left) asked me if I was okay. Col's me mate! Is Geoff Boycott (right) congratulating Snowy?

Over the years, however, the more I played against England, the more I concluded that not only did we know as much as them about cricket, we also played it more positively. Lots of Pommy cricketers are regarded as great 'thinkers' about the game. Still, ninety per cent of players with a reputation of possessing a great cricket brain are duds with the bat and ball, so I reckon it's better to be seen as having an ordinary cricket brain. It means you're probably an exciting, genuine player. Brett Lee and Andrew Symonds are never perceived as great thinkers about the game, yet quite possibly they are!

Anyway, I'm getting away from the meaning of the Ashes—and the winning of that urn. I mean, we're no longer convicts, but we're still better than the screws at their game—it's a bit like

Who needs the Barmy Army's humorous, harmonious jingles: we've got an inane chant 'Aussie, Aussie, Aussie…

Burt Reynolds's team of prison inmates in *The Longest Yard*. And it's alright to have one solitary inane chant of 'Aussie, Aussie, Aussie! Oi! Oi! Oi!'. You don't need a massive compilation of sixty witty, humorous, philosophical harmonious jingles like the Barmy Army. It's okay to answer the stirring 'Land of Hope and Glory' with 'Waltzing Matilda'—a dirge about a sheep thief who commits suicide. It's alright to have Lleyton Hewitt's manners, Anthony Mundine's mouth and Shane Warne's history of indiscretions. As long as we've got the Ashes, that's all that counts in life. It may seem narrow, but given the size of the cricket community and the history of its participants, it counts more than anything else.

THURSDAY, 23 NOVEMBER 2006

RICKY PONTING MAKES A STATEMENT ON DAY ONE

The Queensland Cricket Association's First Test Breakfast on the opening day at the Gabba is always an appropriate lead in to any international season. This morning, I'm the keynote speaker and the punters have given me a generous ovation. Mind you, the audience is so fully pumped by the Ashes contest just a couple of hours away that Peter Costello delivering a Budget speech about aged care would have drawn applause. Nasser Hussain, the former England captain, is interviewed on stage and attempts to blame others for his decision in a previous Gabba Test to send Australia in to bat only to be soundly thrashed. It didn't wash with most—and, as well, old Nass is losing his hair! If the Anzacs had receded as quickly at Gallipoli as his follicles, they wouldn't have lost a man!

Soon I'm in the ABC box and there is so much expectation I thought Glen Mitchell would give birth before the toss.

'Punter' Ponting was a man on a mission during this series—the ghost of the 2005 Ashes loss had to be busted. 'Freddie' Flintoff never gave up, but by the end of the First Test 'Punter' had a very firm grip on the urn

Ricky Ponting has won the flip and chosen to bat—advantage Australia. Steve Harmison charges in for the first ball of the series and bowls a quick one! Andrew Flintoff takes the pronounced outswinger at second slip but, sadly, the only thing it hit during its journey was the outside of the return crease! Only Mal Meninga's political career started as poorly.

Matthew Hayden and Justin Langer had survived a pre-series boot camp. The pies that Messrs James Anderson and 'Harmy' were serving up are received far better than cold baked beans and a soggy Anzac biscuit. Eventually, with the total on seventy-nine in the nineteenth over, Flintoff accounts for Hayden.

In marches captain 'Punter' Ponting, a man with a mission. He has thought of nothing else but regaining that little urn for fifteen

Ponting was in the form of his life in this Test—the best in the world

months—the ghost of the Ashes loss in 2005 had to be busted—and he is in the form of his life from the outset. The front foot is moving quickly and decisively into position, and his forward and backward defensive shots seem like mandatory foreplay before the real humping start. Punter isn't singling anybody out for special treatment. All fruit is dealt with without favour—whether it's the pear-shaped Ashley Giles or the apples and plums of Matt Hoggard.

Ponting is the best batsman in the world on this form. His exhibition of front foot on-driving is the most brilliant I have ever witnessed. I've been lucky enough to see the likes of Greg Chappell, Doug Walters, Steve Waugh and David Boon break bowlers with their on-driving. Ponting, on this bright Brisbane afternoon, makes that quartet look as banal as a Darwin weather report. 'Freddie' Flintoff is the Poms' best bowler. He is very physical. Never gives up—and asks more questions in one hour than Eddie Maguire. Punter is walking off at stumps with 137 not out against his name. He has the look of a man who wants to double that tomorrow. His team is 3–346 and 'Mr Cricket' Mike Hussey is at his captain's side with sixty-three not out.

How good would it be to have Mr Cricket alongside you in war? He's so nice, however; he'd want to discuss surrender with the enemy over a cup of tea. This day, however, belongs to the boy from Mowbray—that urn has already requested a change of ownership form.

Ponting's 196 steered Australia to a first innings total of 602. From that lofty position the home side dominated the match, eventually winning by a massive 277 runs. The Punter had one hand on the Ashes … and it was a very firm grip at that.

When he's not crunching fours, 'Mr Cricket' Hussey runs between the wickets like Forrest Gump on steroids. Out of the way umpire Rudi Koertzen!

TUESDAY, 5 DECEMBER 2006

THE UNWINNABLE GAME— GO WARNEY!

On this same day in Brisbane in 1928, express bouncer/chucker Harold Larwood took eight wickets in the match to star in England's victory over Australia by a mammoth 675 runs. Could this be an omen? Andrew Flintoff's team has pole position in this encounter.

This is the last day of the second Test and I'm in Sydney— curiously. I've never called an Adelaide Test for the ABC. I don't know why. Maybe it's because I have stated publicly on occasions that ninety per cent of Adelaide males part their hair down the middle and have at one stage contemplated knocking off their neighbour and storing him in the garage in a garbage bin full of acid. Management can be so sensitive, can't they?

Still, England has played well on Les Burdett's well-manicured lifeless strip. Burdett is so good at making things behave well he could cultivate calm in Oasis on tour, I reckon.

The Poms made a mammoth 6–551 in their first innings yet lead by only ninety-seven runs with nine second innings wickets in hand as the fifth day begins. There are parochial whispers that if Australia can apply early pressure then England may take the gas.

By lunchtime, a gas truck has, in fact, ram-raided the English dressing-room! It emerges, when the dust has settled, that their mindset has been all wrong. Ashley Giles—who struggled to make any impression on the series—wrote on his website that day of waking up and feeling incredibly nervous. Feeling something could go wrong despite his team's sound position, 'Flash Ash' went to the hotel gymnasium in a bid to exercise the negativity out of his body. He remarked how other team-mates

Ashley 'Flash Ash' Giles celebrates dismissing Adam Gilchrist, but he had a lot to make up for; dropping 'Punter' Ponting cost his team a few hundred runs

who were also in the gym had given him the same impression. Nobody had spoken very much, but everybody seemed to have a common thought: there's every chance we could bloody well stuff this up, mate! And stuff it up they eventually did.

Shane Warne would have rolled out of his queen bed that morning, put away five or six cigarettes and a toasted cheese sandwich. And then declared, 'The Poms will shit 'emselves today if we get a couple of early wickets'. Warne always cuts to the chase.

The day's cricket is more incident-packed than a night out with Ben Cousins.

A wretched decision by umpire Steve Bucknor to rule Andrew Strauss out caught close in started the surrender, and the needless run out of Ian Bell saw two wheels and a few nuts and bolts fall off the Pommy cart.

Flash Ash Giles, though, could make up for all his previous sins in the match—notably the dropping of Ricky Ponting on the square leg boundary, which had cost his team a few hundred runs. The Englishman has some tasks ahead with ball and bat on this last day and he should be up for them. Though he spins less than a cannon ball, Ashley can block! He can keep a harmless half-volley out of his stumps better than any number eight batsman of his era. In fact, Giles could defend better than OJ Simpson's lawyers. This was the ideal situation for him. An hour or so of rigid defence and England could walk away from the city of churches only one down on the series.

At 6–94 the English lead is 134. Twenty or so from Giles and a partnership with Paul Collingwood and they may salvage a nervous draw. He has already soaked up fourteen minutes at the crease when Warne decides to come around the wicket. Warney could write cricket's *Karma Sutra* he loves variety so much. From this altered angle of release the Australian champion has often produced incredible sleights of hand. In tennis these moments are known as the big points—and Warne has an impressive history of winning them. The next Warne delivery pitches a foot outside leg stump and Giles, looking to play off the back foot to give himself more time to adjust his shot if the ball misbehaves, is squared up—exposed. The outside edge is taken and Hayden neatly pockets the catch to his right at first slip. This is Warne's genius. Rocking back on my lounge, I murmur, 'Australia will piss this in'—succinct if not erudite. As a fellow leg spinner, this wicket does as much for me as the ball of the century to the hapless Mike Gatting all those years ago. I think my first-class wicket tally was 486. I wish just one had been taken this way.

Warney's just jaffa'd 'Flash Ash' Giles. He loves variety so much Warney could write cricket's *Karma Sutra*

England loses its last nine wickets for a paltry seventy and Ponting's men need a potentially uncomfortable 167 to take a 2–0 lead.

The captain smacks five boundaries, Damien Martyn plays a loose shot and promptly retires—talk about marking yourself hard—but Mr Cricket (Mike Hussey) crunches fours and runs between the wickets like Forrest Gump on steroids. Amid unprecedented scenes of emotion, Australia takes a six-wicket win after tea. This game was both unwinnable and unlosable. The Aussies achieved the first and the Poms the latter. But the delivery at the heart of it all was the Warne 'jaffa' to Giles.

Despite four days of media criticism that this pitch was too benign to produce an exciting climax, Curator Burdett was given a standing ovation when he walked into the Members' area for a post-match beer. Adelaide Tests always produce something.

ABC Radio has rostered me to call my first this summer. Apparently all those jibes at South Australians have been forgiven. I'll have to think of some more!

THE ASHES RECLAIMED! ...
BY MY ROOM-MATE

The Ashes are regained in Perth on 18 December 2006—yet another triumph for the Australians, particularly Ricky Ponting, who played a crucial part in the victory with his expert captaincy and a timely seventy-five in the second innings.

The match is even more significant for me because I roomed with Warney. Well, I didn't exactly share the same room with him but when I checked into our East Perth self-contained apartment block on the eve of the match I was in 316 and I shared a common door with the occupant of 317. That afternoon as I entered my room the door of 317 was ajar and smoke was coming from it. I thought immediately 'Oh no, I've drawn a smoker', whereupon a mop of blond hair appeared.

'Hi Skull, come in,' extended the great leg spinner. If you're going to inherit a smoker as a neighbour, he may as well be the best damn cricketer in the world. It's like going to a golf driving range and the guy next to you is called Tiger.

Immediately I was drawn into the Test team inner circle of card players. Warney loves Texas Hold'em Poker and he was jousting with Stuart Clark, Andrew Symonds, Glenn McGrath and a couple of his Hampshire county team-mates. The Poms were looking so lovingly towards Warney I thought they would kiss him when he won a hand. Nonetheless, it was great to be there with that mob and they were welcoming. Andrew Symonds even got my air-conditioning working when I complained that I couldn't get it started. 'Symo' doesn't regard the media too highly so this was indeed a gallant gesture.

I could sense Warney wasn't enjoying his cricket much as we talked around midnight over the next three nights between hands of cards and toasted cheese sangers. His marriage and escaping the scrutiny of the Australian media seemed to be his priorities. I sensed there was an imminent announcement about his playing future.

His room was interesting. There were dozens of cans of baked beans and a single block of cheese in the fridge. And, yes, enough cigarettes to have satisfied the tobacco rations of the Anzacs over two world wars.

On the second night he said, 'Help yourself to something to eat, Skull.' Well, there was only a loaf of bread, the baked beans and cheese in his larder. A limited buffet you'd have to say. Throughout the night, Warney was Warney—aggressive at the card table, self-deprecating when he wanted to be and comfortable with team-mates around him. It was obvious that his team-mates enjoyed his company and, moreover, he enjoyed theirs. The sanctity of the dressing-room is everything to many players. It's Warne's cave. The outside world can pass him by when he's bunkered down with his junk food, fags and his mates.

A senior Victorian cricketer, who played a number of seasons with the champion, once told me that nobody has ever seen Warney pissed. It's an amazing revelation—and un-Australian. The leg spinner likes to keep his wits about him, according to former team-mates.

Symonds is much loved. It's his honesty and his forthright humour and perhaps a certain lack of worldliness which captivates those around him. It is little wonder that Ricky Ponting and a couple of other senior players wanted him in the team for so long despite frequent modest statistics.

When Andrew Symonds fixed my air-conditioning I didn't match his celebratory style!

McGrath is respected. He's the old voice. He's been around, he's done so much. The farmer's son from Narromine, in country New South Wales, has done pretty well. It's been suggested that his rural property portfolio is so large he could form his own state west of Orange.

Clark, too, is well liked. He's no shrinking violet when it comes to an opinion, but he's respectful and only pipes up when asked. Warne likes him and has invited him to play with Hampshire this winter. This sort of invitation doesn't go to mugs. Clark read my first book and said he enjoyed it. I reckon he's going to get 1000 Test wickets on that compliment alone.

It was great rooming with Warney. Occasionally I'd open my door and there would be, on the floor, a can of baked beans that had dropped off his shopping trolley. And there was always the

Stuart Clark said he enjoyed my first book—that guarantees him 1000 Test wickets! He'll certainly take many

smoke emanating from under his door. It was so bad, in fact, that I had to stuff towels under *my* door to stop it from creeping passively into my room. That guy could smoke for Australia.

I've always liked him. He's always been pleasant and welcoming. This match wasn't one of his best with the ball, though he did take four wickets in the second innings. Funnily enough, Perth's never been really kind to Warney, but when the Ashes were there to be won and the Aussies were just one wicket from the regaining of same, it was fitting that Warney there was with a viper to knock back Monty Panesar's middle stump.

Back in the motel room I was preparing for the red eye special (the midnight flight from Perth to Sydney). I heard Warney enter the common hallway. It was late. The players had been celebrating in the rooms. The stench of nicotine and alcohol

Warney loves a send-off—if only photographs could speak! And what a roomy. What a guy

invaded our little corridor. I was going to knock on the door except I think he was showering. I knew that the boys had been out that night. The security guards and plain clothes detectives were with them. They had every right to celebrate—you don't regain the Ashes every day and it was right that the boys should have a real craic around the nightspots of Perth. I sensed Stuart Clark had had enough of celebration, but in the Aussie tradition he felt he had to go out and he did. He's such a team man, S Clark.

I caught that midnight plane back to Sydney. This flight, at my age, is having a craic as well! It takes you all the next day to recover so what's the point in catching it? It's a myth. My roomy Warney is no myth, however. What a guy!

WEDNESDAY, 20 DECEMBER 2006

LUNCH WITH 'KOFO'

I have a strong preference for lunching over doing dinner. I have long preferred to drink alcohol responsibly in the daylight—always have. With a longish lunch, you inevitably have an early night—sometimes very early. Greybeards reckon that the hours of sleep before midnight are the most beneficial of all.

The week preceding Christmas is a particularly pleasurable five days of lunching. It has a sort of Mad Monday attraction for me—a let-your-hair-down exercise after the main business of the calendar year has been completed. In recent years, as my life has taken a turn for the better, I have organised luncheon engagements in the Christmas week. Today is a particularly great day for good food and good wine.

The venue this year is Machiavelli—a downstairs Italian restaurant in Sydney's Clarence Street. By reputation, the antipasto and spaghetti are among the top seeds among this fair city's nosheries.

I am the guest of Paul Kofod, a former Eastern Suburbs Roosters rugby league lower grade player, who talks like a leaguie but who apparently went to a private school. It's not obvious at first sight. 'Kofo' has that touch of South Sydney larrikin. He is as earthy as Bulli soil and, significantly, seems to have risen to reasonable heights in the Commonwealth Bank. It is my second visit to Machiavelli. Kofo has the air of a season-ticket holder. We are seated at one of the premium tables in the front of the basement under a giant photograph of Frank Lowy. I have one of the wealthiest men in Australia—I think he's seeded second behind James Packer—over my right shoulder. Frank's face seems amiable enough, though as the main man of Westfield Holdings and given that I've been in enough of his shopping centres to have chatted to a few of his tenants, I'd rather have him on a wall behind me than deal with him directly in rental negotiation. They say he drives the hardest of bargains.

The last time I was at this restaurant I had the former premier, Sir Robert Askin, above me on the wall. Old Sir Robert was something of a scallywag with whom justice never seemed to catch up. Still, he was an avid supporter of the Manly Warringah Sea Eagles and that, to this Dragons' supporter, was a form of weekend detention in itself.

Back to the food. It is well above average. Kofo is doing all the ordering and getting it so right. He's chewing on the Fusilli Crab—there's so much chilli in it he won't get a cold for six months! I've chosen the Pepper Steak and although my opinion might be clouded by my grape intake, I reckon it's as good as I've had anywhere in the world. More bottles of expensive red are requested and duly given a seeing to. Dessert is contemplated.

My traditional favourite is Tiramisu but the table advises that there are better options.

I've already chalked up two visits to the bathroom. All this wine is playing havoc with my bladder. I'm off for a third trip to the men's. It is a nasty twenty-five yard traverse past legs and arms. I stumble. Damn it. I'm pissed! The attention of other lunchers is caught by my rather laboured gait returning to the Kofod table.

Machiavelli is as much about who dines there as the food. It's inappropriate to stare too long at somebody you recognise, so there are any number of half glances at the Sydney political and corporate heavies who seem to use this tuckshop regularly.

Kofo continues to entertain with his waggish view of life— particularly sport, business and women. His brother, Mick, is a financial guru. Kofo suggests we three go to a Roosters match in a week or so. I hate the Roosters, but I'd go to see them lose. My condition deteriorates further when the port arrives to complement the cheese platter. Suddenly we seem to be the only table occupied. It must be passé to do long lunch at Machiavelli's. Kofo settles the account but not before someone utters the obligatory 'anyone for a couple of cleansing ales?' My record for saying 'Yes' to this enquiry is 2580–0. Make that 2581–0!

Just around the corner from our restaurant is the Occidental Hotel in York Street. It is old style: stained carpet, low ceilings and the overhanging haze of cigarette smoke. My late and great father used to drink here regularly when he worked for Allan Kippax Sports Store after its relocation from Martin Place to York Street. The Occidental serves Reschs beer. I now only drink Reschs—and draught Reschs at that. I had secretly reached a decision on alcohol. My days of drinking canned or bottled beer have come to an end at fifty-six. It's keg beer or nothing for me from now on. The schooners of Reschs are going down a treat. After four I have considered the ale to have cleansed me.

Kofo is a responsible drinker. He calls time on us and it's time to fall into a taxi. I'm on my way home. I'm safe but wounded. Dinner for me will be a hot shower and a litre of water. In bed at 7.45 pm, you beauty, I'll wake up fine. And there're still four days till Christmas. Hope Kofo rings tomorrow.

ANOTHER ABC CRICKET SUMMER ENDS

The summer is officially over. England has surprisingly lifted its form and won the VB Series 2–0 against Australia. The Barmy Army numbers are much diminished, but those that were in Sydney last night for the finale would have thoroughly enjoyed Freddie Flintoff's squad's triumph.

Sadly, there will be no more ABC Cricket commentary for the season. It's both a relief that the travel has finished but a regret as commentating on the national broadcaster is one of my great passions. I've been doing it regularly now since 2001 and I look forward to every day in the box. People say to me how lucky I am to do it for a living. Well, it's not quite a living, it's more like five or six Tests a year. But I agree. It's the best seat in the house and it satisfies my thirst for this great game.

Having done a lot of public speaking in recent years, and been nervous at every single engagement, my mindset for radio cricket is in stark contrast. I would not know how many people are listening to the coverage via the national broadcaster, but I don't feel any nerves before or during my commentary stints.

As the players file onto the field, or when I take up one of my on-air shifts, I have the view that I'm going to discuss the match as I would talking to somebody over a beer in a bar. My overall aim is to bring the cricket to the audience, but I get distracted. I can fly into left field quicker than a Sammy Sosa home run. I love left field. It's my left field offerings that are so often brought up when I meet listeners as I go about my daily life.

Of course, there are critics who carp when I depart from cricket-speak—those who say that I stray too much from the actual game and that my sniggering gets on more nerves with each passing year. My outlook on why I laugh so much is this: if we can convey in the commentary area that we're enjoying the game then those going about their business tuned to ABC Cricket will pick up on it and ride with it. Fortunately, there are enough listeners out there who enjoy my style.

Perhaps one reason listeners sense that we are having a good time in the commentary box is that we actually are. There is a genuine lack of ego and no elitism among the broadcasters, and when you're locked in an uncomfortable broadcasting box for seven hours a day this helps. I don't know why they build radio boxes so small, but negotiating your position in the commentary area, when knees and ankles and hips are always going at different angles, continues to be a problem as I age.

Our executive producer at the ABC is Caroline Davison, a wonderful operator. She's known as 'Princess Grace' because of her likeness to the style and dignity of Grace Kelly. She seems to have been with the ABC forever but is a strict disciplinarian—good taste and the charter are everything to her. I have been the recipient of a number of yellow cards from her over the years. She's yet to deliver a red. If Grace were a soccer referee, players would be carted off with broken legs, yet the transgressor would remain on the field. That type of officiating suits me. Her dedication to the job, and the manner in which she deals with high-pressure situations is like a beacon. She exudes a calmness that takes over the room. Long may she stay in charge of our cricket.

Caroline draws up the rosters for each day one hour before play begins. It's a twenty-minute stint for each ball-by-ball commentator and half-hour stints for the colour commentators. Our chief ball-by-ball men are Jim Maxwell, who came up during the Alan McGilvray era, and Glen Mitchell, an intense teetotaller from Perth who married the beautiful Karen Tighe. Maxwell and Mitchell have differing styles. Jim has a voice roasted over a burning fire, while

Jim Maxwell came up through the Alan McGilvray era and has a voice roasted over burning fire

Glen has a forthright delivery and a style that highlights the amount of work he puts into preparation for each day's commentary. Some of my funniest moments have been with Glen. He tends to lead me into things and can provoke an aside that breaks us both up.

As I travel the country, the most frequent observation from the punters about our commentary is that they sense our love of the game, and that this in turn draws out their interest and affection for the game. From a professional broadcasting point of view there are Mitchell and Maxwell, and then there is me! Strangely, it has surprised my wife and me and my close friends that my profile is as high as it has ever been because of ABC Cricket. I travel Australia extensively and the greatest satisfaction I get is when people come up and say how much they enjoy ABC Cricket. It's not an ego thing, there is the odd person who comes up and says how much he dislikes it, but the entertainment that we are providing for people throughout the season appears to outweigh the complaints of the dissidents. The critics have forecast there will be a use-by date for my style of commentary—and I can't disagree that there will come a twilight when I may not be as novel—but I feel that after five summers I'm gaining more credibility each year.

I love working with the overseas commentators too. Jonathan Agnew from England still can't come to terms with the fact that I know more about his career than he does, and any reference to his lovely wife still draws a comment like, 'Oh my God how dare you say that about my wife'. Heh, heh! But I love him dearly.

This summer Harsha Bhogle is here with the Indians and if I had a dollar for every time somebody came up and said, 'I love the work you do with Harsha,' I'd be a rich man. Perhaps it's the

I love working with overseas commentators like Jonathan Agnew, seen on air here with self-confessed cricket tragic, John Howard

Harsha Bhogle with former Test opener Keith Stackpole. If I had a dollar every time someone's told me how much they enjoy my sessions on air with Harsha then I wouldn't need to punt!

different senses of humour that bond us; Harsha is so Indian and so straight in contrast to this quirky tongue-in-cheek Aussie larrikin. I don't know whether Harsha understands where our repartee is going on occasion, but he has a wonderful way of responding that has won favour with the listeners.

Fazeer Mohammed comes out whenever the West Indies team is touring. He is a man of great integrity, a practising Muslim, whose love of the game and knowledge of it is a terrific base to work around.

When the South Africans visited a couple of years ago, Zolani Bongco was their representative on ABC Cricket and I reckon my time with Zolani was as personally rewarding as any in recent times. Although he was homesick for most of the trip, this gentle former boxer was intrigued at the style of ABC Cricket and, although initially apprehensive, his enjoyment of our quirkiness deepened with every match.

If there is one co-commentator I just haven't been able to gel with, it is Brian Waddle of New Zealand. I don't know what it is about 'Wadds'. Either he doesn't get my stuff or he gets it and doesn't rate it. I still haven't quite worked that one out. It may be that he's upholding all that is good about New Zealand cricket in the face of these over-confident, cocky Australians. Sadly, I've never developed any rapport with the veteran Kiwi broadcaster in the two or three summers that I've worked with him. Still, I'm not giving up. I'm determined to crack a Waddle smile by the end of our radio career together! It's my broadcasting Shangri-la.

ABC listeners, however, are my priority, particularly those in regional Australia for whom Aunty is such an important outlet. Whether they are farmers driving headers, or country people going about their working lives in utes, they are my principle focus as I broadcast. If there is a cocky trapped in a tractor from 6 am to 6 pm in outback Bourke, I want to make their journey through the day as entertaining as possible.

When we broadcast from the major grounds, there are a number of individuals and groups who brighten our day with their gifts. Every day of the Sydney Test the Loftus Primary School mothers deliver a freshly baked cake to the broadcasting box. Their orange and almond offering on day one of the Ashes Test last summer was to die for—and their standards for a number of years have been as high as any three-star Michelin chef. And in Sydney, too, there's the lobster that arrives each second day, courtesy of insurance agent Michael Whetton from Wollongong. Michael has been driving freshly caught lobster up the Princes Highway now for three or four years. This followed my bitter complaint that we had to do better than the milk arrowroot biscuits for afternoon tea. Hearing that whinge Michael jumped into the ocean off Wollongong at first light the following morning, caught two lobsters, boiled them, put them in ice and drove them to the SCG and presented them in the commentary area. The Bradman Stand chef then put them on a lovely platter with dressings and fresh salad and we had the most magnificent seafood at afternoon tea. It has become a Sydney Test institution. I don't request it any more because when I did the first time a senator drafted a stern email about the open solicitation of lobster on the national broadcaster and sent it to ABC management. You've got to be so careful on Aunty! Nonetheless, once fresh lobster enters the commentary area it's like gannets around a feast.

You discover a great deal about human nature when such delicacies are on offer. Peter Roebuck, in particular, will risk

When delicacies are on offer in the commentary area, Peter Roebuck will risk serious injury to get to the lobster tail

serious injury in his enthusiasm to get to the lobster tail. It's a disadvantage to be on air when Michael's lobster enters the room. Occasionally I have been involved in the tea time summary when the feeding frenzy has begun and had to settle for dipping lettuce leaves in thousand island dressing for my portion. Still, I'm a selfless man these days!

I've never had a contract with the ABC and it's unlikely that I'll ever be asked to sign on the dotted line. A phone call from head of sport, Peter Longman, in mid-winter is about as formal as my arrangement gets. Hill will send me a commentary roster for the summer and request that I reply about my availability.

Another season has gone. There are just seven months of footballers apologising for their weekend behaviour on Monday television before I saddle up again. Roll on November!

22–23 MARCH 2007

THE PURA CUP FINAL …
TASMANIA AT LAST!

I'm watching the Pura Cup final from Bellerive Oval in Hobart and I'm captivated. I love State cricket when it's all on the line.

The Tasmanians are attempting to win their first ever domestic four-day competition. They are in the final and they're hosting on a belting pitch in front of their long-suffering supporters. The crowd is growing by the day, as you'd expect it to—they're on the brink of history. Tasmanian administrators have been great supporters of the Australian Cricket system but have just a couple of limited over triumphs to boast about over the years.

The Apple Islanders have a great opportunity in this match as they lead by 336 runs going into the fourth day. Luke Butterworth looks a very impressive young player—a left-handed batsmen who bowls nippy medium-fast pace. At only twenty-three years of age this fellow has a future—a big future! Butterworth has done well in the one-day format but has yet to establish himself in the four-day game. Sometimes sleepers like Michael Hussey emerge after a number of years of anonymity, Butterworth may just be the latest. Technically he looks the goods. He uses the crease well, watches the ball on to the bat, works clinically through mid wicket, and he's just hit MacGill for a one-bounce four over deep mid wicket. It appears as if once he picks his ball he can hit it a long way. Yes, I like the cut of this young man's jib. All the talk is about Andrew Symonds or Shane Watson being the all-rounder in both forms of the game over the next few years, but this Luke Butterworth is not without a puncher's chance of developing into an alternative for either the Australian Test or one-day teams.

New South Wales is under the pump here. It's day four and this pitch is giving them not too much less than it did on the previous three days.

Matthew Nicholson's done well with the ball. He possesses an imperfect action and appears to try to swing it against his body momentum. 'Nicho' has the biomechanics of an inswing bowler yet moves it away from the right hander. He's just signed a contract with Surrey to play county cricket. It's not his first season in the English game but he's always wanted a career as a professional cricketer. This fellow from Knox Grammar School in Sydney has worked at his game and won respect. He's striving away against Sean Clingeleffer and Butterworth. Traditionally Tasmanian players seem to utilise a great number of letters of the alphabet in their surnames; Clingeleffer, Kremerskothen and Polkinghorne are three that spring to mind. I don't know how Jamie Cox got in there—just three letters in his surname—he might be Coxascoffen or Coxaloffer but he managed to shorten it somehow.

I'm looking at the New South Welshmen. Grant Lambert, the

Tasmania has a 'no dickheads' policy … This team plays for each other

Blues all-rounder, looks like the kind of guy—with a Best Bets hanging out of his jeans pocket—who'd be in a packed TAB most Saturday afternoons, ducking out occasionally for a ciggie. He's dominated District cricket in Sydney for so many years and here he is, finally comfortable at the next level. Lambert batted well—he got sixty-odd not out in New South Wales's first innings—he'll need to get runs in the second.

'Stuie' MacGill is such a talent. He's still got the leg spinning viper and he's moving well in the field. I saw him in the previous game—his work at mid-on makes Phil Tufnell look like Mark Waugh—but he looks free of injury today and his pursuits have been much more athletic. He's got to fill the void next summer with the retirement of Shane Warne because the gap to the next best is just too far.

Stuart MacGill has such talent. He's the next best bet for Life After Warne

Blues off spinner Nathan Hauritz is an interesting bowler. He's taken his first class wickets at an average in the high fifties—but he's better than that. His trademark is to bowl good deliveries that don't get people out. Oh, and perhaps he doesn't spin it all that much either. It's just that he has the straightest of bowling arms. I reckon he could do with another nine per cent bend in his right elbow.

Nicholson's bowling splendidly. He's got a Malcolm Marshall quality about him. Occasionally he gets one to really take off. His deliveries are a little like Elton John—they can go either way! There's a bit of a private school element creeping in to New South Wales Cricket. Nicho's an old Knoxian and Ed Cowan is an old Cranbrookian. I don't know about Cranbrook. Some of their old boys have not exactly distinguished themselves in recent times.

A cynical mate of mine once cracked that 'economics in Year 12 at this Eastern Suburbs' school could be known as tax evasion'. He was just kidding, I'm sure!

I'm watching the final on Fox. I'm addicted to sport on cable television.

The Pura Cup final is being played in working hours from Monday to Friday. Rupert Murdoch calls the tune in summer as much as he does with his coverage of the Australian Rugby League competition in winter. Nonetheless, I love watching the next tier of players and Rupert allows me to see them live from my lounge room. I've come to appreciate the Fox commentary team. Cricket commentary is not a walk in the park, particularly on television where technology rules. I much prefer radio where you can venture into left field with your thoughts without a director steering you back to what's on the screen. Technique is everything in calling cricket on television. Nobody has really tried to clone the Richie Benaud style where you let the picture completely tell the story. Less is best with Richie. A number of the Fox commentators still fall into the trap of describing each delivery as if they were calling to a radio audience. I'm impressed with the professionalism of the coverage nonetheless.

Brendon Julian is a comfortable fit as host. He's cricket's male version of Jennifer Hawkins. Good eye candy and dozens of white teeth. He could be American for all we know!

Allan Border has always been a good bloke and is a much underestimated commentator. His analyses over the years have always been on the money. Yeah sure, his delivery may be a little bland but it's what 'AB' says that is particularly significant. I appreciate his sentiments. He has undoubted credibility having scored around five million runs under pressure throughout his playing career. As a commentator AB never tries to be anything he isn't—he's just himself.

Mark Waugh is at his most amusing when he's not trying to be amusing. 'Junior' is an unspectacular commentator; however—given that he didn't want to be a Test selector and was quoted as saying he would get bored stiff having to watch cricket all day—it's interesting to see him embark on a career covering cricket where he has to watch it ... all day. Make sense of that! Mark's knowledge of the game is obvious, which is refreshing, yet his delivery is criticised as being a little too one dimensional. However, many lounge-room punters regard him as the silkiest player many of them have ever seen. That alone will be enough to win support.

Back to the cricket: Doug Bollinger is bowling well. His left-arm pace is much admired by people in high places, particularly David Boon who has been waiting for some time for Bollinger to establish himself at first-class level. He reminds me of the former giant from New South Wales, Phil Alley, who promised much in the '90s for New South Wales without really delivering. It's a shame because he was a decent fellow who probably should have played basketball given that he was a few metres tall.

Bollinger has impressed me in the first innings of this match and I've got the feeling that he will challenge Mitchell Johnson over the next couple of summers for a spot in the Test team. He's come from park cricket without a solid grounding in the specifics of the game. Insiders said that when he initially arrived at District cricket level he was ordered to go to third man and

Doug Bollinger's left-arm pace is much admired. He has the look of a good neighbour, the kind who would mow your lawn as well

had to ask where it was! His fielding is a little sluggish and will have to be addressed over the next period of his career, and his batting is a cross between Glenn McGrath and Stuart Clark. Dougie has the look of a good neighbour—somebody who would not just mow his own lawn on a Sunday but would probably cut yours as well.

Butterworth continues to bat with impressive acumen; his work through cover is clinical and pure. He finds a lot of gaps as well, rarely finding the fieldsmen when he's looking to hit the ball to the boundary.

Tasmania has all but wrapped up this match. New South Wales will be set too many to get on the last day. The locals deserve this victory. Their bowlers have been the key throughout the season. Tassie selectors decided to base their campaign around a four-pronged pace attack and it has borne a rich dividend.

Their main man has been Ben Hilfenhaus, a brickie's labourer who has an uncomplicated action and who can bend the ball like Beckham. Hilfenhaus has put New South Wales away with an inspired spell on this last morning. Bowlers who can alter the path of the delivery once it's left their hand are gold. Richard Hadlee and Dennis Lillee are two greats who were pretty handy at changing the direction of the ball mid-flight. Hilfenhaus has been bowling New South Wales out all season—twenty-odd wickets against them at an average of around thirteen is some kind of a stranglehold on one team. The New South Wales coaching staff will have to address the techniques of their batsmen against the moving ball before they can be confident against the likes of Hilfenhaus. Cowan chopped an inswinger into his stumps with feet nowhere. Lambert slashed a moving delivery to slip and Thornely was bowled by an inside edge late on the shot with feet pushing across the crease, while Katich pulled a bouncer straight to the man at square leg. These were all dismissals which had a technical flaw at the base.

These Tasmanians are a mixed and interesting collection of fellows. Their coach, Tim Coyle, has embarked on a 'no dickheads' policy in recruitment and fostering, and appears to have come up with an ideal list. Damien Wright is the son of Geoff, a formidable Sydney District player in the '70s who went on to become a bookmaker and a low-handicap golfer. Wright junior smiles all the time and looks the most genuine of young men. He is possibly the best bowler to left-handers in the country and has been for some seasons. For a man with such a sweet nature, he still knows how to winkle out the better batsmen. Michael Di Venuto has served Tasmanian cricket with aplomb for a number of years. The don of Italian cricket, Simone Gambino, was desperate to sign up 'Diva' to lead the Italian charge towards the World Cup, but when the ICC brought in the rule that to play for one of the minnows you had to be born in the country, it ruled out the hard-hitting left-hander. Tasmania has been the beneficiary. His straight play at the top of the order has been a real factor this summer. He deserves this title having played in previous final losses.

There are others equally as deserving. Formidable men like Michael Dighton, who came over from Western Australia and has been a big part of the team's success; Travis Birt, a slogging left-hander who has done well in county cricket but will have to tighten his game before he becomes a Michael Hussey. At the moment he is looser than Mikey Robins's belts.

George Bailey is a very interesting player. He has a private-school look about him possibly because, I've just been informed, he went to a private school. He is a very inventive batsman with a sound temperament and he's going to play a huge part in Tasmanian cricket during the next decade. A source close to the Tasmanian camp told me last year that George is likely either to captain Australia at cricket or be a future Prime Minister.

Daniel Marsh has led from the front and fully deserves this Pura Cup title. He is the son of Rodney and Roslyn and has got much of his father's dash and his mother's attention to detail. His father was more spur of the moment and intuitive.

Sean Clingeleffer deserves special mention for his fighting century. A scoreboard's nightmare with so many letters of the alphabet in his surname, he deserves this triumph. Apparently he was dropped earlier in the season but recalled, as much because of his popularity among his team-mates and their desire to see him be part of this triumph as anything else. Everybody apparently loves 'Clingy' and he has not disappointed with perhaps a career-best performance with the bat.

The umpires have had good games. Bob Parry has impressed with a number of correct lbw decisions and Rod Tucker, a former New South Wales and Tasmanian player, is not far from international umpiring.

The Pura Cup has been won by the best team. The Tigers led the competition from the outset. They have the right culture, the right coach, the best pace attack in the country, and youth. Their victory is as much a triumph for their undying support of the Australian cricket system as anything else. Go you good things!

Damien Wright (centre)
celebrates taking another scalp
in the Tassie Tigers title win

Tasmania v. New South Wales
Pura Cup 2006–07 (Final)

Venue Bellerive Oval, Hobart, on 19, 20, 21, 22, 23 March 2007 (5-day match)

Balls per over 6 • **Toss** Tasmania won the toss and decided to bat

Result Tasmania won by 421 runs

Umpires RL Parry, RJ Tucker • **Third umpire** BNJ Oxenford • **Referee** RT Widows

Scorers JC Gainsford, GW Hamley

Close of play day 1 Tasmania (1) 283–7 (Butterworth 40*, Wright 57*; 90 overs)

Close of play day 2 New South Wales (1) 207–8 (Lambert 43*, Bollinger 3*; 70 overs)

Close of play day 3 Tasmania (2) 203–6 (Clingeleffer 8*, Butterworth 22*; 82 overs)

Close of play day 4 New South Wales (2) 3–0 (Jaques 3*, Lambert 0*; 1 over)

Man of the Match LR Butterworth

Tasmania first innings		Runs	Balls	Mins	4s	6s
MJ Di Venuto	c Smith b Lambert	24	49	73	4	–
TD Paine	b Bollinger	0	3	9	–	–
MG Dighton	c Smith b Bollinger	33	74	112	4	–
TR Birt	lbw b Nicholson	32	33	37	6	–
GJ Bailey	c Smith b Bollinger	1	12	21	–	–
*DJ Marsh	c Hauritz b Bollinger	44	92	131	8	–
+SG Clingeleffer	c Thornely b Bollinger	41	97	108	5	–
LR Butterworth	c Smith b Lambert	66	139	195	8	–
DG Wright	c Cowan b Nicholson	67	105	131	9	1
AR Griffith	c Smith b Lambert	19	40	60	1	–
BW Hilfenhaus	not out	0	6	9	–	–
Extras (5 b, 4 lb, 3 nb, 1 w)		13				
Total (all out, 443 minutes, 107.5 overs)		340				

Fall of wickets: 1–2 (Paine, 1.5 ov), 2–44 (Di Venuto, 16.2 ov), 3–84 (Birt, 24.4 ov), 4–90 (Dighton, 27.2 ov), 5–94 (Bailey, 29.3 ov), 6–173 (Clingeleffer, 57.2 ov), 7–188 (Marsh, 61.2 ov), 8–299 (Wright, 94.4 ov), 9–335 (Butterworth, 105.5 ov), 10–340 (Griffith, 107.5 ov)

New South Wales bowling	Overs	Mdns	Runs	Wkts	Wides	No-Balls
Nicholson	23	8	66	2	–	–
Bollinger	26	6	73	5	–	1
Lambert	20.5	2	87	3	–	1
Thornely	7	2	21	0	–	1
Hauritz	7	1	22	0	1	–
MacGill	24	3	62	0	–	–

New South Wales first innings		Runs	Balls	Mins	4s	6s
PA Jaques	b Wright	82	169	229	10	–
EJM Cowan	b Hilfenhaus	17	32	39	3	–
*SM Katich	c Clingeleffer b Hilfenhaus	4	9	11	1	–
DJ Thornely	c Butterworth b Hilfenhaus	41	80	105	6	–
BJ Rohrer	lbw b Butterworth	1	9	13	–	–
+D Smith	c Bailey b Butterworth	5	21	31	–	–
GM Lambert	c Wright b Butterworth	61	74	110	10	–
NM Hauritz	c Marsh b Wright	1	13	12	–	–
MJ Nicholson	c Marsh b Wright	2	17	26	–	–
DE Bollinger	c and b Butterworth	6	31	44	–	–
SCG MacGill	not out	1	1	3	–	–
Extras (7 lb, 2 nb)	9					
Total (all out, 312 minutes, 75.4 overs)		230				

Fall of wickets: 1–40 (Cowan, 10.3 ov), 2–48 (Katich, 12.6 ov), 3–137 (Thornely, 38.4 ov), 4–141 (Rohrer, 41.3 ov), 5–155 (Smith, 49.5 ov), 6–169 (Jaques, 56.1 ov), 7–171 (Hauritz, 58.4 ov), 8–197 (Nicholson, 64.3 ov), 9–229 (Lambert, 75.2 ov), 10–230 (Bollinger, 75.4 ov)

Tasmania bowling	Overs	Mdns	Runs	Wkts	Wides	No-Balls
Hilfenhaus	25	4	88	3	–	–
Griffith	16	2	63	0	–	2
Wright	15	5	38	3	–	–
Butterworth	16.4	6	33	4	–	–
Marsh	3	2	1	0	–	–

Tasmania second innings		Runs	Balls	Mins	4s	6s
TD Paine	c Hauritz b Nicholson	5	13	18	1	–
MJ Di Venuto	run out (Lambert->Thornely)	64	107	164	9	2
MG Dighton	c Lambert b Nicholson	10	20	32	2	–
TR Birt	c and b MacGill	28	105	147	5	–
GJ Bailey	lbw b Lambert	50	107	124	5	1
*DJ Marsh	c Cowan b Nicholson	7	47	63	–	–
+SG Clingeleffer	lbw b Thornely	107	304	419	6	–
LR Butterworth	b Hauritz	106	194	230	15	–
DG Wright	lbw b MacGill	47	88	127	4	1
AR Griffith	c Hauritz b Thornely	3	27	41	–	–
BW Hilfenhaus	not out	7	8	7	1	–
Extras (11 b, 5 lb, 10 nb)		26				
Total (all out, 686 minutes, 168.2 overs)		460				

Fall of wickets: 1–19 (Paine, 3.6 ov), 2–49 (Dighton, 10.1 ov), 3–107 (Di Venuto, 36.3 ov), 4–117 (Birt, 45.2 ov), 5–157 (Marsh, 62.4 ov), 6–176 (Bailey, 68.1 ov), 7–339 (Butterworth, 126.1 ov), 8–432 (Wright, 157.5 ov), 9–453 (Clingeleffer, 166.3 ov), 10–460 (Griffith, 168.2 ov)

New South Wales bowling	Overs	Mdns	Runs	Wkts	Wides	No-Balls
Bollinger	25	6	66	0	–	–
Nicholson	31	7	92	3	–	–
Lambert	17	2	73	1	–	5
Thornely	18.2	10	23	2	–	1
Hauritz	27	7	56	1	–	–
MacGill	49	9	133	2	–	4
Rohrer	1	0	1	0	–	–

New South Wales second innings		Runs	Balls	Mins	4s	6s
PA Jaques	lbw b Griffith	5	7	4	–	–
GM Lambert	c Marsh b Hilfenhaus	18	32	43	3	–
EJM Cowan	b Hilfenhaus	7	11	14	1	–
*SM Katich	c Paine b Hilfenhaus	34	34	58	6	–
DJ Thornely	b Hilfenhaus	0	5	10	–	–
BJ Rohrer	c Clingeleffer b Wright	30	55	79	4	–
+D Smith	b Wright	7	16	27	1	–
NM Hauritz	c Clingeleffer b Wright	0	9	15	–	–
MJ Nicholson	lbw b Wright	28	26	34	3	1
DE Bollinger	lbw b Wright	12	17	22	–	1
SCG MacGill	not out	1	1	3	–	–

Extras (2 b, 1 lb, 4 nb) 7

Total (all out, 154 minutes, 34.5 overs)   149

Fall of wickets: 1–5 (Jaques, 1.3 ov), 2–13 (Cowan, 4.2 ov), 3–36 (Lambert, 10.2 ov), 4–52 (Thornely, 12.1 ov), 5–69 (Katich, 16.6 ov), 6–94 (Smith, 22.6 ov), 7–104 (Hauritz, 26.3 ov), 8–115 (Rohrer, 30.1 ov), 9–148 (Nicholson, 34.3 ov), 10–149 (Bollinger, 34.5 ov)

Tasmania bowling	Overs	Mdns	Runs	Wkts	Wides	No-Balls
Hilfenhaus	11	4	22	4	–	–
Griffith	9	0	62	1	–	4
Butterworth	4	0	19	0	–	–
Wright	6.5	3	13	5	–	–
Marsh	4	1	30	0	–	–

Source: Courtesy of cricketarchive.com

TOM BECOMES A NATIONAL CHAMPION

It's a Sunday morning and I'm home alone. I've just returned from a few days away working in regional Western Australia. I'm nervous. My youngest son, Tom, is competing in the Australian Surf Championships in Perth. Because of my work commitments I've been unable to get to these titles but have had regular bulletins from Scarborough Beach about how they are going.

Tom has made the final of the Under 17 Surf Race event. It will be the first on the day's program. He has put a lot into his preparation—my son trains six days a week; he does eight to ten sessions in the Carss Park pool under the tutelage of well-regarded swim coach, Dick Caine. This means, as all swimmers know, getting up at 5.10 am, five mornings a week and going back at least three or four times for extra sessions in the afternoon. He develops his skills on the Malibu board at Elouera

Surf Club a couple of times a week, and trains to sharpen his speed with notable conditioners like Jock Campbell and Paul Watson on the sandhills of Wanda.

Tom is a committed athlete. So far this surf season in competing for Elouera the major titles have eluded him. At the District championships and again at the State titles he led the field in his pet event, the Under 17 surf race, but has been run down by competitors catching late waves from behind him. This is not an uncommon frustration of surf racing. Competitors term it being 'jagged on'. Every competitor has, at some stage of his career, been jagged. Tom was disappointed at a couple of the losses: in the New South Wales Championship final he led the swim some fifty metres from the beach only to be becalmed in dead water while three of his competitors caught a wave to relegate him to fourth place. Encouragingly he took the disappointment as motivation and intensified his training for these Aussie titles.

The first couple of days have gone well. With his good mates Rory Gillespie and Dane Farrell he won gold medals in the Under 17 Cameron Relay and the Under 19 Board Relay. Sharing accommodation with his mother, and being able to eat well-prepared meals, had him in the pinkest condition. My wife has confided to me that on the eve of the final Tom had made a significant comment when he stated, 'Mum, in previous years at Aussies I've been intimidated but not this year. I don't feel intimidated by anybody.'

Tom is one of the favourites for today's final. He qualified for the final via the heats, quarters and semis, and looks most impressive from all reports. However, all his main adversaries would be on the starting line this day. Kendrick Louis, a very fine surfer from Collaroy; Luke Cole from Cronulla, a gifted young athlete with whom Tom has had many tussles in the last two or three years; Saxon Bird from Queenscliff, who's always been around the money; Dean Mackay from Avoca and Tim Schofield from Terrigal would also be in the final with better than a puncher's chance.

There had been the odd prayer for Tom in the O'Keeffe home in the weeks leading up to these titles. My wife had prayed more for luck than anything else because she knew deep down that Tom had put in the hard work to get into this position, and luck, of course, is a huge factor in surf racing. Nothing worthwhile has ever been achieved without sacrifice, and all those thousands of laps in the pool before the sun came up was the price the majority of the finalists will have paid.

The Scarborough surf this day was apparently relatively flat. There was a shore break but not too much else. These were conditions that would suit Tom, who is a strong swimmer and may just be able to pinch a yard if it came down more to swimming ability than wave craft. My wife rang as they were assembling on the starting line. I could sense nervousness in her voice. She really wanted this for Tom as much as anything in his short life. It would not have mattered if he'd finished a long last today, but she longed for him to taste a victory for which he'd worked so assiduously. I, too, working at my desk, felt the nerves.

Apparently he got a good start, always a problem area—you might think it is the finish that counts, but each surfer needs to get off the beach—and he was cutting with the leaders halfway out to the cans. At the markers Tom had a lead, if only slight, from Kendrick Louis, and Luke Cole was just off their shoulders. The local swimmer Tom Darling from the City of Perth was in their wake, as was James Taylor from Redhead and an unknown Dev Lahey from Sunshine Beach. Not much was known of Lahey but halfway back to the beach he hit the lead.

I'm at home awaiting the call. It came. I could hardly decipher what I was being told. Tom had caught a wave with Lahey and Louis but ridden it an extra stroke, giving him a yard advantage up the beach which he held to the line. All hell had then broken loose. Elouera is known as the family club and has not tasted too much success in recent years. Officials and fellow team-mates were all over Tom. His mother was blubbering. She'd fallen into the arms of Carol Gillespie, Tom's best mate's mum. They were

Son Tom's words, 'Thank you for taking me to the pool all those mornings, Dad', after he won the Australian Under 17 surf title, broke me up

crying together. I was fielding the phone call. Tears welled in my eyes as she said Tom had won the Australian Under 17 surf title. I know how much it meant to him. I was just so proud. There are moments in a father's life where the feeling of pride for your offspring is boundless. This was just such a moment. Not for boasting rights but for the fact that he put in such an effort and he'd found reward.

Within a few minutes Tom was on the phone and his first words after I congratulated him were, 'Thank you for taking me to the pool all those mornings, Dad.' It broke me. In his victory he'd had the clarity of mind to thank me. But this was Tom's day. He'd beaten Lahey into second place and Louis had taken the bronze. Since then I've seen the photos of them on the dais. I've seen the photo of him crossing the line where he just lifted his right hand and the index finger to suggest number one. It was his first win of the year but it was in the most prestigious event on the most important day. My Tom, the little 'Spider', was an Australian surf champion.

On Tom's return to Carss Park, coach Caine told him that whatever else happened in his life they would never be able to take away that he was the best in the country for his age in the surf that day.

Every father has these sorts of days, those moments when your heart bursts with pride for what an offspring has achieved. This was just such a day!

AUSTRALIA LOOKING GOOD FOR THE WORLD CUP FINAL

W e've been holidaying in Noosa for three days and already the charm of this quaint beachside resort has de-stressed us city folk.

It's midnight and I'm under a blanket watching game eleven of the Super 8 on cable television. Australia is taking on England, who must win to stay in semi-final contention. The match is being played in Antigua—where Brian Lara managed his Test world record—at the Sir Vivian Richards Stadium. Curiously this bland oval gives quite the opposite appearance to the man after which it was named. There was nothing pedestrian about 'Smokin' Joe' Richards. I played against Viv on many occasions and suffered on a majority of them, but occasionally I would pick his wicket. Viv, you see, always liked to work leg spin against the turn through the on side. In a one-on-one duel with Shane Warne, though, my money's on the blond. Still, I digress.

The pitch is flatter than Shane Watson's stomach. Australia is in the field and Shaun Tait has taken the new ball. As a flat slinger Tait wants to bowl on pitches with carry. And he's got one here. He's sending down missiles at speeds of around the mid-140 kilometres per hour. The Australians have not felt the absence of Brett Lee during the tournament with Tait going so well in his place. Nathan Bracken is bowling from the other end. There isn't much swing in the West Indies, though Bracken has been one of the most economical bowlers in all of Australia's lead-up games. It's a measure of Bracken's standing in the game that he manages to keep it tight and still get people out in the form of the game, despite not being able to move the ball through the air too much.

Michael Vaughan is opening the batting for England. He's a very good captain but I feel that he's not a shadow of the player he was

Michael Vaughan is a very good captain, but not a shadow of the player he was in Australia a few years ago

in Australia in 2002–2003. He's had knee problems and there is a stiffness and lack of fluidity in his stroke play. He doesn't seem to pick the ball up as quickly as he did and it's not surprising that Tait goes through him with pace early on. Tait slapped one in—it was quick—but Vaughan was in no position to play the ball and edged it into his stumps. He was late on the shot, as he has been over the last few months whenever I've seen him bat. Vaughan hasn't got a century in eighty-three one day internationals. They can't justify him going in at the top of the order every game anymore.

Tait's bowling action does not flag longevity—it's low and flat and places heavy emphasis on a shoulder thrust, but his strength and youth are currently his great allies. The Aussie selectors have a dilemma. They must use Tait extensively now, for the fear is he may not be bowling at this sort of pace in five years' time. The benefit of Tait's extra yard of pace is obvious again when Andrew Strauss chops a snorter onto his stumps.

Here comes Kevin Pietersen. He averages fifty-six in one day internationals at a strike rate in the eighties. I've never met him but the mail is he's not the sharpest knife in the drawer. I don't think he really cares about how he's perceived, he's out to carve himself a career as one of the finest players of all time in an England shirt and he's making a pretty good fist of it. The cameras happen upon Prince Harry, who is watching his beloved England from a private box. That kid doesn't lead a bad life. When he came to Australia recently he seemed to just nightclub his way around the country. Here he is in Antigua, sucking on complimentary rum, with a delicious blonde on his arm while hobnobbing with the royalty of West Indian cricket. People say it's difficult to be a blueblood, that it's not the easiest of lives. Yeah right!

Kevin Pietersen and
Adam Gilchrist collide.
Pietersen was playing
well, striking over and
through long-on as clean
as a Shannon Lush floor

Glenn 'Pigeon' McGrath has come on to bowl and the English
batsmen are attacking him. There's no movement for Pigeon off
the pitch or through the air and Ian Bell, in particular, has
decided that they're going to take to this aging champion. His
body may not be what it was, but McGrath is driven, as Steve
Waugh was, by pride as much as any other motivation. As an
observer I sense that all opponents plan to attack McGrath from
the outset in every match. With that in mind it might be worth a
trip to the local sports betting outlet to see how much he is
showing for leading wicket-taker in the tournament. To get the
better of McGrath the risk must be that you take him on the up
because his trajectory is so set. Today, though, there is no
movement and he's only bowling in the low 130s. Bell has
decided that he's going to hit on the up through the line at every
opportunity. At the other end Pietersen is playing Michael

Clarke's left-arm orthodox spin very cleverly as well, striking it over and through long-on as clean as a Shannon Lush floor. From nowhere he'll produce a sweep. He's a very dangerous player.

Andrew Symonds has been introduced and there is neither bounce nor movement off the seam for the burly Queenslander. There is a suspicion that his right shoulder is not as strong following a quick recovery from injury, and Adam Gilchrist is now standing up to the stumps to him. Both Bell and Pietersen have completed half-centuries. They look dangerous. Bell's left elbow is higher than a Lindsay Lohan blood alcohol level. High left elbows turn me on, always have! Pietersen has just been dropped by Matthew Hayden. It looked a simple chance to mid-off off the splice but Hayden appeared to be looking where Brad Hogg was running from mid-on. At the peak of his form he doesn't need a collision now with the big matches just around the

Flat slinger Shaun Tait was sending down 140 kph missiles against England, whose batters tried to collar ageing champion Glenn 'Pigeon' McGrath. More often than not they failed

corner. Hayden may have made a meal of the catch but having read his latest cookbook he does a mean chicken cacciatore.

Tait has been recalled. He's bowling really fast and none of the Englishmen look comfortable against him. Having met Taity during a brief visit to New Zealand at the end of the Australian season, I find no correlation between the mild-mannered, respectful Adelaide boy with whom I spoke in a hotel foyer and the snarling, grunting resentful intimidator who takes the new ball for his country. But that is the way of cricket. You can't be self-effacing and reserved and still take the new ball for your country. It's just not the way of the cricket world. Tait plays his role to perfection.

McGrath has just dismissed Bell slicing a drive to cover point. The Australians needed that wicket. Paul Collingwood's come in. The Aussies believe that he nicks more than Norman Gunston and is a little vulnerable to sledging. Shane Warne had a real go at him about receiving an MBE for scoring seven runs in the 2005 Ashes series, and it seemed to get under his skin. Top-class cricket is such an elitist arena: anybody who is perceived as just a scrapper is more vulnerable to cynical mouthing than the royalty of the game.

Tait has been brought back and straight away Collingwood nicks to Gilchrist just as Australia thought he might. This has been a good ploy by Ricky Ponting. A photo had appeared in the previous weekend's Australian newspapers which suggested that Punter might have been a little affected by alcohol on that evening. Nobody has ever said that Australian cricketers have to lead the lifestyle of Trappist monks.

Andrew Flintoff is at the crease—he's desperately short of runs—and his work on a pedalo at 4 am a couple of nights previously while full of rum is still fresh in everybody's mind. On ya, Freddie! A sighting of Flintoff with a bat in his hand is the cue for Brad Hogg to hand his cap to the umpire to begin a spell. From the way Flintoff attempts to figure out the vagaries of Hogg, you could be forgiven for thinking that the only Chinaman Freddie has ever seen brought a chow mein and fried rice to his table a week or so ago. On cue Hogg spins a wrong 'un past the bat and then almost immediately tries another googly which Flintoff advances to, misses by two feet, and is stumped. People talk about Flintoff being one of the great all-rounders. When you misread spin as much as Freddie Flintoff does then you are a long way short of greatness. He's a fighter. He can strike it long on his day, and he's a bowler of some substance, but he's not in the highest echelon of all-rounders. Not yet anyway.

Ravi Bopara has come in. He looks like Younis Khan. Have those two been seen in the same room? Tait's reverse swing is worrying him. Despite imploring umpire Rudi Koertzen for lbw decisions with his reverse swinger, Tait is missing leg stump by too far to get support from the crusty South African. Rudi is getting it right on these occasions.

England is running out of overs and their main man Pietersen is approaching a century, but he's not hitting enough boundaries. This is a belting pitch and Australia will work out a very high par score. When Australia is playing their best limited over cricket they very often dry their opponents up late in the innings making boundaries hard to come by. Their main method is for their quicker men to bowl full, and force batsmen to take a risk across the line. Bopara holes out to deep mid wicket off Bracken. Despite his hair, Bracken is again impressive. There are a few

Bracken wigs in the crowd. 'Bracks' is from the Blue Mountains and straight hippy-length hair to the middle of your back may still be in vogue there. He has bowled his overs conceding a miserly 3.7 runs an over on this very good pitch.

Pietersen has a well-deserved century. He's celebrating with hands aloft. I sense that his team-mates aren't as happy for him as they may have been—they're a little distant. I get the impression that he still has work to do to be genuinely loved within that England dressing-room. Maybe it's the South African in him. But as a batsman he's strong down the ground and inventive to boot. Eventually he falls to Bracken, striking one low to long-off.

Saj Mahmood has come in and got out almost immediately. Call me a harsh judge but I can't see what this fellow offers with the bat, the ball or in the field. A mate of mine reckons that the England selectors are a pack of poofs and they just love perving at the swarthy Saj! It's a left-field theory and I'm not going with it.

Paul Nixon can slog and he duly hits McGrath out of the park. Because he has a lot to say the Australian players don't seem to like him much, but this bald wicket-keeper is not there to win popularity polls among his opponents. He's there to keep his team upbeat. He perishes, caught in the deep in the quest for quick runs. You sense England are thirty or forty under par here. They had to get more boundaries in the middle and didn't after the thirtieth over—that's a credit to Australia and to Ponting.

In the end a total of 248 is okay, but the greybeards would have you believe it's still under par on this quality pitch. Australia walked off the field as a unit, with very positive body language. I suspect they thought they should have been chasing 280, so they're happy with their morning's work.

Hayden and Gilchrist have gone out to open the Australian innings. Hayden is the leading run getter in the tournament and he looks in great touch. Word has it that twenty-four hours before the game he'd spent considerable hours batting against the bowling machine set up in the middle of the ground. Hayden loves to sit down in the lotus position inside the popping crease and visualise where the bowlers arm will be coming from during his innings come match day.

England needs early wickets. James Anderson is crucial. Despite his ability to swing it both ways there is an imprecision about Anderson which is a concern for coach Duncan Fletcher and captain Vaughan. If the ball is not moving, as so often happens in the West Indies, he can be vulnerable.

In the first over Gilchrist is almost bowled by an inswinger from Anderson. Now that *did* swing! Over the years bowlers have thought their best method against Gilchrist was to swing it back into the left-hander, but if you get it wrong you disappear regularly through the leg-side. This Anderson delivery, though, was precise and cruised past the off stump. To be successful against Australia on good batting pitches bowlers need to be able to change the course of the ball in flight. It should become a priority for every opponent of Australia over the next few years to foster bowlers of this ilk.

Hayden should have been out lbw in the first over; although he was a long way down the pitch the ball would have hit the stumps. Anderson is aggrieved and umpire Billy Bowden has got this one wrong. Australia gets a lot of these. I sometimes think that officials may be intimidated by the Australians—the world's number one team — and as a result they win far too many 50–50 decisions from international umpires.

Mahmood has come on. His first ball is a low full toss which Gilchrist caresses to the cover boundary. Mahmood, as you may have guessed, is not my favourite cricketer but he should have had Gilchrist out lbw next ball. Rudi Koertzen again rules in favour of the Australians when the ball was going to hit middle stump about halfway up. The miracle from my point of view is that you could actually miss a delivery from Mahmood. Okay, admittedly its 4 am Queensland time and I'm a little tired, but I reckon I could do a fair job facing Mahmood if we were to confront each other out the front of my apartment.

Hayden is starting to drop kick the ball over deep mid wicket for regular boundaries. Flintoff has come on and Gilchrist has been caught immediately. Freddie may be having an indifferent World Cup but he can still take the big wickets. Ponting is in and moving crisply into his work—Neil Harvey couldn't have been better on his toes than the little Tasmanian. Ponting is without question the finest player in the world at the moment and his footwork against Monty Panesar is a delight. Punter is a driven man during this World Cup. Every time he comes to the crease his body language screams that this is all about a ruthless and clinical retention of the trophy. No stone is being left unturned.

Michael Clarke is in at number four after Hayden departs for forty-one. He has now undoubtedly secured this spot in the batting order. His busy working of the ball is not producing many boundaries, but it allows cricket enthusiasts to marvel at his Dean Jones-like ability to scamper between the wickets. Eventually Ponting is run out for eighty-six and a bristling Symonds enters to club twenty-eight not out from just twenty-eight balls to take a seven wicket victory. England now cannot and do not deserve to

'Punter' Ponting was a driven man during the World Cup, his body language at the crease screaming clinical retention of the trophy.

Monty Panesar with his left-arm tweakers has added an extra dimension to England's attack

make the semi-finals. Their bowling is just too fragile against the better sides. Australia has the momentum. It has continued to pick the same team throughout the tournament and that appears to be the policy leading to the final in Barbados. I feel I have watched the cup winners throughout the night; now I'm off to grab a couple of hours' sleep before hitting the waves of Noosa.

Australia v. England
ICC World Cup 2006–07 (Super 8)

Venue Sir Vivian Richards Stadium, St Peter's on 8 April 2007 (50-over match)
Balls per over 6 • **Toss** England won the toss and decided to bat
Result Australia won by 7 wickets • **Points** Australia 2; England 0
Umpires BF Bowden (New Zealand), RE Koertzen (South Africa)
Third umpire Asad Rauf (Pakistan) • **Referee** MJ Procter (South Africa)
Fourth Official NA Malcolm • **Man of the Match** SW Tait

England innings		Runs	Balls	Mins	4s	6s
IR Bell	c Hussey b McGrath	77	90	126	9	–
*MP Vaughan	b Tait	5	8	12	1	–
AJ Strauss	b Tait	7	10	11	–	–
KP Pietersen	c Clarke b Bracken	104	122	182	6	1
PD Collingwood	c Gilchrist b Tait	2	5	3	–	–
A Flintoff	st Gilchrist b Hogg	4	19	20	–	–
RS Bopara	c Hussey b Bracken	21	36	43	2	–
+PA Nixon	c Hodge b McGrath	8	6	14	–	1
SI Mahmood	c Hodge b Bracken	0	2	2	–	–
MS Panesar	not out	1	2	3	–	–
JM Anderson	lbw b McGrath	0	1	2	–	–
Extras (4 b, 4 lb, 3 nb, 7 w)		18				
Total (all out, 49.5 overs)		247				

Fall of wickets: 1–10 (Vaughan, 3.2 ov), 2–24 (Strauss, 5.6 ov), 3–164 (Bell, 29.3 ov), 4–167 (Collingwood, 30.3 ov), 5–179 (Flintoff, 35.3 ov), 6–230 (Bopara, 46.2 ov), 7–240 (Pietersen, 48.4 ov), 8–240 (Mahmood, 48.6 ov), 9–246 (Nixon, 49.2 ov), 10–247 (Anderson, 49.5 ov)

Australia bowling	Overs	Mdns	Runs	Wkts	Wides	No-Balls
Bracken	10	1	33	3	1	–
Tait	10	0	41	3	3	2
McGrath	9.5	0	62	3	1	–
Clarke	4	0	27	0	–	–
Hogg	10	0	36	1	1	–
Symonds	6	0	40	0	–	–

Australia innings		Runs	Balls	Mins	4s	6s
+AC Gilchrist	c Collingwood b Flintoff	27	37	51	5	–
ML Hayden	b Collingwood	41	50	91	6	–
*RT Ponting	run out (Collingwood)	86	106	133	11	–
MJ Clarke	not out	55	63	130	2	–
A Symonds	not out	28	28	33	4	1
MEK Hussey	did not bat					
BJ Hodge	did not bat					
GB Hogg	did not bat					
NW Bracken	did not bat					
SW Tait	did not bat					
GD McGrath	did not bat					
Extras (1 b, 5 lb, 5 w)		11				
Total (3 wickets, 47.2 overs)		248				

Fall of wickets: 1–57 (Gilchrist, 10.6 ov), 2–89 (Hayden, 19.1 ov), 3–201 (Ponting, 40.1 ov)

England bowling	Overs	Mdns	Runs	Wkts	Wides	No-Balls
Anderson	10	1	49	0	3	–
Mahmood	9.2	1	60	0	1	–
Flintoff	10	1	35	1	–	–
Panesar	9	0	48	0	–	–
Collingwood	9	0	50	1	1	–

Source: Courtesy of cricketarchive.com

TUESDAY, 10 APRIL 2007

THE O'KEEFFES GO
TO THE ZOO

It's a balmy Tuesday in Noosa and the temperature is expected to get into the mid twenties. The water temperature is around the same so there's no difference between sitting on the beach and swimming. I like that in a holiday resort.

We come to Noosa on the Sunshine Coast of Queensland every April for our annual holiday. I can't take holidays in December or January because of cricket broadcasting commitments, so it's really good to be here with the family when the numbers aren't as great as they are over the Christmas–New Year break.

Noosa is delightful. This beach has to be as good as any in the world when it's in its full pomp! In previous years we've stayed at Dennis Weight's unit at Noosaville—a village less than ten minutes from Noosa main beach. Weight was the physiotherapist for well over a decade with the West Indian cricket team. He now lives on the Gold Coast with his West Indian wife and four children under the age of ten. Good luck, Den! His superannuation package is the Noosaville unit.

This year however we're staying on Hastings Street at the French Quarter. It's our first venture into living close to the heart of Noosa and it's working out. For the first time in eight years our oldest boy Dan will not be with us. He has university commitments and a girlfriend, and at eighteen perhaps he may have outgrown the family holiday. I'm saddened by it, but that's life. Tom, our younger boy, is with us and this year he's brought up his Malibu board and his surfboard. Consequently we've driven from Sydney with the surfcraft strapped to racks on top of the car.

Every April I attempt to launch into a fitness campaign and it normally begins with 6 am runs through the National Park on Noosa Hill. I love these runs. Well, they're not really a run, more of a shuffle. Sometimes seventy-five-year-old retirees walk past

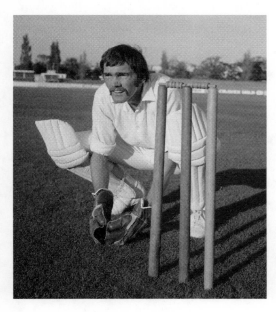

Richie Robinson was a pretty good 'wicky', and a neatness freak. He kept his protector in a mohair bag ...

me even though I'm attempting to run—it's embarrassing, but I soldier on. After completing the five-kilometre run I walk into Noosa to get a newspaper.

This morning I'm accosted on Hastings Street by a fellow in a white bakery T-shirt and shorts. He jumps out at me from behind a shopfront. It's Richie Robinson, my wicket-keeper throughout the 1977 Ashes tour and World Series Cricket, and a pretty good 'wicky' to boot. He was always as fit as a fiddle and a neatness freak—even his protector had its own mohair cover in his cricket bag—but it was his batting and his energy at the crease which marked him apart from a number of his contemporary wicket-keeper/batsmen. Richie and I had shared a number of batting partnerships throughout our period together. He was always great to bat with because he was the aggressor. He looked to take the initiative from the moment he came to the crease. After gathering myself from the initial assault he tells me he's got a bread run (Monday to Friday), has settled in Noosa where he's always wanted to live, and just loves the place. He goes on to say that he stays as fit as he can by doing an hour's workout on the beach every day after work.

Within two hours my wife and I are on the beach and there is Richie striding through the surf towards Noosa groyne, thighs pumping.

Tom is off for the day. He has his Malibu board and he's searching for waves down at the river mouth. I love spending time with my wife Veronica on these holidays. She's fantastic company, so rational. I bounce my harebrained ideas off her constantly and she modifies and analyses them. In all our twenty years together she's never condemned or criticised any of my strategies, though we've only ever applied about ten per cent of them after discussion.

Despite almost a decade of trips to this part of the world we've never been to the Australia Zoo, the late Steve Irwin's grand project. It's at Beerwah about forty-five minutes south of Noosa. Veronica and I have decided that with Tom off surfing we should take the opportunity to visit it. On arrival— entrance is $45.00 per person, I'm glad Tom didn't come—we discover we're just in time because there's going to be a croc feeding. We take our place in the stands and Terri Irwin appears. She's in khaki, as her late husband always was, and she's joined by a fellow named Wayne who has a special relationship with Graham the saltwater crocodile they're about to feed. Wayne was with Steve on the night Graham was caught, and before the croc finally submitted he took a hunk out of Wayne's thigh. The daily feeding of crocodiles appears to be dangerous work, even more so when you throw yourself into the nearby pool, as Wayne does, and then escape as the crocodile moves swiftly towards you.

Veronica and I embark on our own tour of the zoo. Suddenly we're in the snake pavilion. I've never liked snakes, perhaps because I'm a city boy. I'm apprehensive even though the serpents are behind strong glass. Irwin has seeded the snakes from one to ten in the category of most venomous in the world and we are in front of the top seed—the deadliest snake of all. It's called the Fierce Snake and I'm reading its biography, which says that one nip from this fellow could kill 100 men. In other words if you're bitten by the Fierce Snake you say goodnight and goodbye within a couple of minutes. Wow! Crikey! It lives in central Australia and the inscription says it's a quiet, gentle private snake, but heaven help anybody who disturbs it.

It's time to go back to Noosa and we're driving down the highway around mid-afternoon. I'm peckish and suggest we should look for a place to have lunch. On the left is the Ettamogah Pub, a strange-looking building with a quirky shape which is something of an icon around the Sunshine Coast. We decide to have a counter lunch there. It's a quaint timber construction with pine floorboards and upstairs is Bluey's Bar 'n' Grill. The blackboard says that its hamburger is the biggest burger ever! Well, we'll both try one. I'm up for a real hamburger having had McDonald's plastic offerings too much on this trip already. I went for the Beef and Bacon Burger—it's the best I've ever eaten—absolutely brilliant. The chips are old fashioned, thick and salty and I'm hoeing in.

An hour or so later we're back in Noosa. Tom asks me if I'd like to have a late swim with him. His form in the surf is far superior to mine, but nonetheless I challenge him to a contest as to who can ride the waves furthest into shore. Severely disadvantaged by weighing forty kilograms more than my opponent, Tom beats me thirty waves to zero. He could ride the ripple off a short soup. As we head for the showers Richie Robinson's back, power walking through the water doing leg raises. That guy is still the Eveready battery man, he just never stops. Noosa at twilight is so pleasant. I shower and lie back watching TV. I feel good. My family is around me—or most of them anyway—and I'm savouring every moment I spend with Tom, who might elect to stay at home next year, who knows? Still eight straight April holidays in Noosa isn't bad—I want to keep coming here forever.

SRI LANKA FIELDS ITS SECOND ELEVEN

Game forty-three of the 2007 World Cup will be important for both teams. A win for Australia will make it almost impossible for New Zealand to finish first in the Super 8 group. A Sri Lanka victory will ensure them a semi-final berth knowing they have only to play Ireland in the final match of this section of the tournament.

The National Stadium at Grenada is hosting the match. I'm watching and the Sri Lankans have already stunned everybody by omitting their two key bowlers, Chaminda Vaas and Muttiah Muralitharan. The excitement machine, Lasith Malinga, is known to have an ankle problem, though there is a suggestion he could have played at a pinch Nonetheless, Tom Moody and his senior advisers have decided to rest their potential match winner. There are bigger fish to fry in a week or so.

Mahela Jayawardene has won the toss and elected to bat.

Sanath Jayasuriya, who forms a
crucial opener partnership with
Upul Tharanga for Sri Lanka

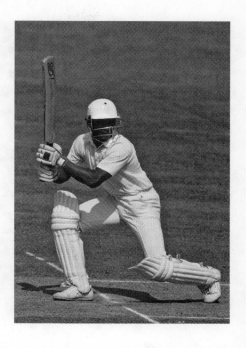

There's notable assistance for the quicker men in this pitch.
Nathan Bracken has got it to swing a little early and Tait is
bowling very fast, if waywardly, and Gilchrist is compelled to do
a lot of recovery work down the leg-side. The Sri Lankan openers
Upul Tharanga and Sanath Jayasuriya are crucial to their team's
tactics. They need to get away as a pair and things look good.
Jayasuriya is moving quickly into his shots. He doesn't seem to be
having a lot of difficulty picking up the action of Tait. This is
something the Sri Lankans believe is not difficult given that they
have a bowler in Malinga, who has a similar round arm-slinging
delivery. Bracken has grown another leg on this tour—he's
moving the ball away from the left-handers. He gets Jayasuriya
with one that goes the other way, trapping him on the half front
foot and winning the lbw appeal from Umpire Aleem Dar.

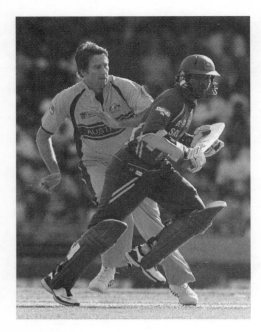

Glenn McGrath is one of the best fielders off his own bowling ever. Here he looks to cut off a single against Sri Lanka

Pigeon McGrath is introduced and begins with his signature metronomic opening over. Almost immediately Pigeon strikes Sangakkara a little high but still wins an lbw decision from Umpire Dar.

Tharanga has had a modest World Cup so far by his standards, but the selectors are bound to back this fine player when the heat is on in the final games. At once, though, Bracken's swing undoes him and he's taken at first slip by Hayden.

At 3–27 in the seventh over Australia has already overturned the disadvantage of losing the toss. The Australian fast bowlers seem to bowl better trajectories than most other quick men around the world. Both McGrath and Bracken are getting the ball to climb past the splice of the bat regularly. This is the defining skill that separates them from so many of the other trundlers.

Even on the flattest of surfaces their pure trajectory is still something that concentrates batsmen's minds.

Jayawardene has come in—he's a class player. He covers the ball with his head more than most players from the subcontinent so the bounce isn't so much a problem for him, and he watches it closely onto the bat. The only other player in World cricket who smells the ball on the bat as much as Jayawardene is Mr Cricket—Mike Hussey.

Chamara Silva and Jayawardene are playing in their wristy manner, turning the bat face, working angles between fieldsmen, but Brad Hogg has been introduced and Greg Blewett has just said in commentary that Sri Lankans play spin well. I couldn't agree less with dear old 'Blewey'. I reckon the Sri Lankans' techniques against Shane Warne and Stuart MacGill in recent years have been despicable.

Hogg is in with a big chance here as very few of them seem to read his wrong 'un. The former postman from Perth has struck an

Andrew Symonds saves twenty runs in the field each innings. He is the best ground fielder I've ever seen

immediate length and is bowling very straight, using his wrong 'un to great effect as expected, but Symonds is leaking boundaries from the other end. Having returned so quickly from his shoulder injury, the Queenslander lacks precision and does not appear to have regained full strength in that body part. Ponting's men need Symonds to bowl well in these vital games because Shane Watson is under an injury cloud, and he and Michael Clarke are going to have to fiddle ten overs between them as the fifth bowler.

The Australian out cricket is outstanding. Already I've seen Hogg chase one that would have been two in any era, and Hussey at deep backward square leg has raced around, intercepted and fired in a return to prevent a second run. It's a contrast between fielding today and yesteryear. Sri Lanka has reached 3–102 in the twenty-seventh over—that's a run rate of 3.78 per over.

The pitch is sluggish but this is still an under par score at this stage of the innings. Neither Jayawardene nor Silva is doing enough yet and Ponting has just taken a power play and reintroduced McGrath. This is the Sri Lankan opportunity to attack Pigeon. I wonder if they will?

The Australian fieldsmen are missing with their underhand flicks at the stumps—you have days when that happens. Hopefully when the finals are being fully waged the Aussie infielders can find the sticks. Jayawardene has drop-kicked McGrath over long-off for a one-bounce boundary and then Silva has plastered Tait through cover for a similar result. Silva is another of the high left elbow ilk and his open bat face is a technical trait of so many from the subcontinent. This partnership is looking dangerous. Gilchrist has come up to the stumps for McGrath and Jayawardene has just used his wrists to flick him over square leg for a boundary. Pigeon won't like that and the trademark shake of the head accompanies the ball going over the rope.

Tait has come on and he's trying to get his reverse swinger going at pace but Jayawardene is so clever when the ball is tailing down leg-side. He has an uncanny ability to help it on its way, and with the man up inside the circle at fine leg that's a sure boundary for the Sri Lankan captain. Jayawardene has just hit Tait into Cuba with a terrific hook shot over square leg to bring up his thirty-eighth one day international fifty. He was named skipper of the year by the ICC last year, although he had a much inferior win–loss record to Ricky Ponting, so obviously there are a number of people in high places who think he's the best tactical international captain in the game. Jayawardene's half-century has been full of powerful hooks. In fact, the Sri Lankan captain uses the hook more than the murderer in the horror movie *I Know What You Did Last Summer*. Jayawardene and Silva are making this a real contest. Suddenly they're starting to play Hogg better, but I still have a suspicion they're not reading him overly well. They've concentrated more square of the wicket and behind the wicket, dabbing and sweeping, and it's worked on this plasticine-like pitch in Grenada.

Bracken is always impressive. I remember back in 1973 Max Walker bowled superbly on just these pitches by varying his pace and his movement, and that's what Bracken has been doing throughout this World Cup. He's added another dimension to his game in the last twelve months. I can't understand why he isn't a stronger consideration for Test cricket, but his work in the one day form of the game continues to be a real plus for the Aussies.

Silva has assayed one sweep too many at Hogg and the top edge has been taken at short backward square leg. The fourth wicket has fallen with the total on 167 in the thirty-eighth over. It's a vital blow.

Tillakaratne Dilshan has come in at number six. He averages just twenty-nine in one day internationals—the gifted right-hander is better than that, but he can self-destruct and the Australians will be looking to put him under some pressure. Even though Jayawardene has been getting runs off Hogg you still get the impression he's not picking the wrist, and the left-arm chinaman is bouncing the ball impressively. Dilshan is not detecting the Hogg wrong 'un either. It comes as no surprise when Hogg eventually spins the googly past Jayawardene's searching bat and Gilchrist completes the stumping with a fine bit of glove work. As an old wrist spinner myself, the sight of a beautifully flighted googly spinning past a groping bat still warms the cockles of my heart. Jayawardene departs for seventy-two and his team are lurching at 5–174 in the fortieth over. With no Vaas, Murali or Malinga there is plenty of work still to be done by the tail.

I don't know how a fella with a name like Russel Arnold is in a Sri Lankan cricket team—it's a little like a Bill Smith playing for the Brazilian soccer team. Immediately he plays down the wrong line to a Hogg wrong 'un. Hogg takes his cap, having completed ten overs and returned 2–35. This uncomplicated man from the West is having a tremendous World Cup. He's even attracted a George B Hogg stand banner, complete with goofy face and protruding tongue.

Tait has been reintroduced with the number seven at the crease. He's going at well over eight an over, but you sense that his sandshoe crusher and his extra yard of pace might be a problem for the Sri Lankan tail. Tait has just slung a 148-kilometre-per-hour bouncer which Dilshan has spooned to Brad Hodge at mid wicket. Arnold has never looked comfortable and finally he succumbs to a Tait bouncer, bottom edging one into his stumps, late on the shot. Ponting has employed Tait cleverly—just as he did Brett Lee for a number of years. Tait provides Ponting with muscle, and so any batsman who is perceived as being a little timid against the extra yard of pace is asked to face the Tait chin music.

Bracken is back and the Sri Lankan tail is not offering much. The left-arm paceman's ability to run his fingers across the seam on these slow pitches is again to the fore. He keeps beating the outside edge of the right-handers' bats with deliveries that are cut across them. Bracken has his third wicket as Hayden takes a good catch at first slip low to his left, with Gilchrist standing on the stumps. These are difficult catches but Hayden made it look easy. For such a big man he is an outstanding first slip. Kulasekara is out for one and the eighth wicket is down for 184.

Malinga Bandara has come in and deposited McGrath high over mid wicket for a stunning six. Bandara is a more than useful cricketer; he bowls brisk leg spinners and toppies and is handy with the stick. A Michael Clarke left-arm spinner suffers the same fate as McGrath, Bandara tagging it over deep mid wicket for another six. This fellow can swipe across the line with the best of them. Maharoof has joined the party, driving McGrath imperiously down the ground for a boundary. He has a considerable reputation as a swiper. McGrath continues to shake his head. It's now part of his personality—every time the Narromine farmer's son is struck for a boundary or beats the bat he shakes his head. Maharoof's next boundary hasn't pleased him either—an inside edge past the leg stump. McGrath is the leading wicket-taker in the tournament, but his mood darkens noticeably when things aren't going his way. On cue McGrath strikes, claiming Bandara, who has spooned a short ball to mid wicket, and the Aussie paceman has his twentieth wicket of the tournament. Nonetheless he doesn't seem pleased. He's not used to being one of the more expensive bowlers in the Australian line-up and he's gone for almost 5.5 runs an over—well above his usual economy rate.

Maharoof continues to swipe high, wide and handsome and has just deposited Bracken straight down the ground for a boundary and follows it up with another four just past first slip's left hand. Sri Lanka will take any runs they can.

Bracken's hair is getting longer and longer. There is a band in it now. It may not please the game's dinosaurs but it hasn't stopped him bowling some jaffas. He completes a four-wicket haul when Symonds catches Maharoof at long-on.

Sri Lanka is all out for 226 in the fiftieth over. It's below par on this pitch, even more so when you consider there will be no Murali or Vaas to defend on it.

The Australian innings has begun and already Hayden and Gilchrist are pinning their ears back. Boundaries are flying off both blades. These two left-handers are having good tournaments as a pair. Hayden has been unstoppable with his slog over long-on, possibly the most dangerous stroke used at this World Cup. No Vaas at the top of the order with the new ball, and only

Hayden and Gilchrist—their muscle at the top of the one-day batting order has been significant

Dilshan, Arnold and Bandara to bowl the spin, has opened the gates for Australia. Nonetheless Arnold's off spin takes two wickets, inducing an inside edge off Hayden for a catch to mid wicket and then trapping Gilchrist lbw with the faster ball.

Ponting has come in and he looks in the best of touch. He's such a clean striker of the ball all around the ground. He reminds me of Doug Walters the way he can pick up the length of the ball on slow pitches so quickly and hook or pull or cut, but then just as quickly sense something is overpitched and drive it back down the ground past mid on. I love watching the Punter bat—he's a little jockey at the crease. He looks the same size as Bradman. But the Don is unlikely to be as well versed in Launceston greyhound form as his look-alike. He could be Walters as well but he's not as good a drinker—that's no shame, there aren't many who are.

Clarke has come and gone. His position at number four in the order is unchallenged. He's a very fine player, but after some lovely cover drives Bandara has him taken at short cover driving on the up at a leg spinner. In strides Symonds, all purpose and bristling biceps. He and Ponting in cahoots represent real problems for the Sri Lankans. Symonds is clubbing the ball down the ground over mid wicket and whipping it past square leg. This pair enjoy batting together—you can tell they're mates. Ponting wanted Symonds in the side a lot more than he had been a year or so ago. Both race past half-centuries.

Sri Lanka is going to lose this. They've played an under-strength team and although Jayawardene has said that they didn't disrespect the game, Australia will take it as disrespect. Ponting has the resolve of an indignant man. He will have taken the resting of their better players as a slight and this will drive him to take as comprehensive a win as his team can manage. At the end the captain is sixty-six not out. Symonds with an unbeaten sixty-three has proven that he is back, and vital at number five.

Australia now looks as if it will finish top of the Super 8s and play the fourth placed team in the semis. This emphatic victory has lifted their run rate, and most of their stars, particularly the batsmen, are in great touch. They'll be hard to beat in the next fortnight. New Zealand is the next opponent in a couple of days, but it's the semi-final and the final that will now consume the team's thinking.

Australia v. Sri Lanka
ICC World Cup 2006–07 (Super 8)

Sri Lanka innings		Runs	Balls	Mins	4s	6s
WU Tharanga	c Hayden b Bracken	6	22	33	–	–
ST Jayasuriya	lbw b Bracken	12	12	21	2	–
+KC Sangakkara	lbw b McGrath	0	4	6	–	–
*DPMD Jayawardene	st Gilchrist b Hogg	72	88	133	5	1
LPC Silva	c Clarke b Hogg	64	107	119	6	–
TM Dilshan	c Hodge b Tait	7	12	13	–	–
RP Arnold	b Tait	3	10	15	–	–
MF Maharoof	c Symonds b Bracken	25	22	40	4	–
KMDN Kulasekara	c Hayden b Bracken	1	5	5	–	–
CM Bandara	c Hogg b McGrath	17	19	23	–	2
CRD Fernando	not out	0	0	4	–	–
Extras (5 lb, 3 nb, 11 w)		19				
Total (all out, 208 minutes, 49.4 overs)		226				

Fall of wickets: 1–26 (Jayasuriya, 4.3 ov), 2–27 (Sangakkara, 5.3 ov), 3–27 (Tharanga, 6.4 ov), 4–167 (Silva, 37.2 ov), 5–174 (Jayawardene, 39.4 ov), 6–178 (Dilshan, 40.6 ov), 7–183 (Arnold, 42.4 ov), 8–184 (Kulasekara, 43.3 ov), 9–218 (Bandara, 48.6 ov), 10–226 (Maharoof, 49.4 ov)

Australia bowling	Overs	Mdns	Runs	Wkts	Wides	No-Balls
Bracken	9.4	3	19	4	1	–
Tait	10	0	68	2	6	1
McGrath	9	1	48	2	–	1
Hogg	10	0	35	2	–	–
Symonds	3	0	15	0	–	1
Clarke	8	0	36	0	–	–

Australia innings		Runs	Balls	Mins	4s	6s
+AC Gilchrist	lbw b Arnold	30	49	65	4	–
ML Hayden	c Dilshan b Arnold	41	30	56	5	2
*RT Ponting	not out	66	80	116	4	1
MJ Clarke	c Dilshan b Bandara	23	31	38	4	–
A Symonds	not out	63	71	66	5	2
MEK Hussey	did not bat					
BJ Hodge	did not bat					
GB Hogg	did not bat					
NW Bracken	did not bat					
SW Tait	did not bat					
GD McGrath	did not bat					
Extras (5 nb, 4 w)		9				
Total (3 wickets, 173 minutes, 42.4 overs)		232				

Fall of wickets: 1–76 (Hayden, 11.5 ov), 2–79 (Gilchrist, 13.3 ov), 3–126 (Clarke, 23.1 ov)

Sri Lanka bowling	Overs	Mdns	Runs	Wkts	Wides	No-Balls
Fernando	6	1	36	0	3	3
Maharoof	7	0	52	0	–	1
Kulasekara	4	0	20	0	–	1
Arnold	4	0	20	2	1	–
Bandara	9.4	0	53	1	–	–
Jayasuriya	6	0	32	0	–	–
Dilshan	6	0	19	0	–	–

Source: Courtesy of cricketarchive.com

MY WORLD CUP
JOURNEY BEGINS

Today is my wife Veronica's birthday. I'm not a romantic so I wished her a happy birthday and asked her to give me a lift to the airport! Just kidding, darling! But this morning I'm off on my World Cup journey. As always, I'm apprehensive. There are 750 in my tour party and I am co-hosting with Merv Hughes. It is an extraordinary number of people to be overseeing but, having enjoyed my sojourn in South Africa last year with 130 tourists, what's an extra 620? Every day will be a challenge, but as Merv said to me when we had a chat about how best to oversee our group, 'Skull, you are a people person, this will be no problem for you'. And he's right, I love meeting people, I love their stories. It's a far cry from when I played where I felt outsiders were a distraction and my tolerance levels were reasonably low.

Qantas flight 107 from Sydney to Los Angeles is going to be a tough leg—it's twelve and a half hours and I am in 54F. 54F is potentially my worst nightmare and, true to form, the very moment the seat belt sign goes off the woman seated directly in front of me eases her seat back so that my knees end up grazing my chin. What can you say? She's paid for her seat as well.

Still, I've already met a number of my group and there are some familiar faces: the connection from Tamworth, New South Wales, the patriarch John Carter and his son Mick. This time they've brought with them the younger son and brother, Rodney, who in his spare time is a regional pilot. The Carters can drink— no, that's a euphemism—they could represent Australia in imbibing. Fellow Tamworthians Warren 'Storky' Williams and David King, a plumber with established form at handling schooners, complete their party. All are assured to enjoy the Caribbean adventure.

Upon arrival in Los Angeles Airport I marvel at how big everything is, how quickly Americans talk, and how many fast food outlets there are. You can get fat walking from Terminal 1 to Terminal 10 at Los Angeles International if you're a little peckish!

We are tired but we still have two more flights this day. Our connection to Dallas Fort Worth duly leaves and I'm sitting next to an interesting fellow, Liam Gidden, a financial planner of some repute from Sydney. Liam is six feet nine inches tall. He is struggling with his economy seat as well, but is anaesthetising himself with multiple Heinekens. The Los Angeles to Dallas Fort Worth flight leg was tolerable and I down my first coffee at the Dallas transit lounge.

The next flight leg is to Miami and I'm seated alongside another interesting chap, this time from Albury, New South Wales. His name is Dave Martin and he runs a bus company. He has a whimsical sense of humour and we agree how big everything is as we look out over Miami. Dave recalled a bus conference he attended in Melbourne where he struck up a conversation with an American woman from St Louis, who also owned a bus company. Dave ventured that he had forty-five buses in his fleet and asked ask how many she had in hers, fully expecting to trail on the first innings by a few hundred. 'I have 14,000 buses in my company,' she replied. I'm afraid Dave couldn't avoid the follow on.

We're staying at the Sheraton Miami Mart Hotel. It's close to the airport. I'm having a good time on the trip already: I've enjoyed meeting a number of my touring party and I'm looking forward to our arrival in the West Indies tomorrow. Working in cricket commentary detaches you from the body of Australians who passionately follow the fortunes of our Test and one day squads. It's therapeutic spending time with these people, seeing how much they enjoy the squad winning and listening to them discuss the wins and losses with such enthusiasm.

On the drive from Miami airport to our hotel I mused at the size of the car parks attached to the numerous supermarkets. Some of them must have been close to 200 acres—at least in the state I was in it appeared that way. You could buy food and its use-by date will have expired by the time you reach your car! Still, its eleven o'clock and I've been awake now for twenty-eight hours straight—I can't sleep with my knees brushing my jowls! I'm looking forward to tomorrow. We're off to Barbados. I haven't been there for twenty-eight years.

AUSTRALIA TAKES ON THE KIWIS IN GRENADA

It's Friday morning around 7 am and our cruise ship the *Galaxy* has delivered us safely to the island of Grenada. We're in port. True to its reputation as the seventh best cruise ship in the world, the *Galaxy* has left nobody desiring more—food for one thing! Breakfast is an extravaganza—one needs to be disciplined. I eat each morning at the Oasis Café and I'm already making my way towards its buffet on the eleventh floor. There are 1500 guests on board and there's around the same number of staff—it's like having a personal manservant. At home my breakfast is normally fruit, toast with honey, and a short black coffee. As I said, discipline is everything when confronted by the Oasis breakfast smorgasbord and I'm as strong willed as the next man. My tray this morning contains french toast with treacle, a four-egg omelette, two bananas, a muffin and a cappuccino. If you let yourself get carried away, you're letting yourself down! Heh, heh, heh!

I'm a little dusty this morning. It was a long night at the poolside bar, but it was a great opportunity to meet more of the punters on my tour, and I'm yet to meet anybody untoward. Last night I did a few beers with Steve Campbell—he's a good bloke. Steve lives at Hervey Bay, Queensland, and apparently received a decent compensation when struck by a police car a few years before. He has a wide knowledge of sport and seems to enjoy my inane jokes. I also met John Traicos and his lovely wife, Annette. They're from Perth. John's a modest, self-effacing gentleman who doesn't look like a world record-holder, but he is! He played for South Africa under Ali Bacher in 1970 against Australia, and twenty-two years and 222 days later he played for Zimbabwe in a Test match at age forty-six—now that's a world record that will never be beaten! John bowled off spin. The adjectives used about his off breaks were 'disciplined' and 'reliable'. They used the same adjectives for me. They're basically euphemisms for 'couldn't turn it in a washing machine'!

John is tremendous company and so rational. I asked him the previous night at 11.30, after multiple Heinekens, why Hugh 'Toey' Tayfield (the best South African off spinner of all time) had been such a champion bowler. Close to midnight he'd given me a detailed mechanical and mental analysis of Toey's strengths, but I've forgotten it! Amnesia caused by fermented hops is the damnedest thing!

Anyway, back to breakfast. A number of my punters are gathering. Australia is playing New Zealand in a Super 8 match. Grenada is known as the spice of the Caribbean and visitors will be enticed by the sweet scents of nutmeg, cinnamon, ginger and vanilla wafting on the balmy breeze. All I can smell along my nasal passages is the froth from so many Heinekens on the previous night. I'm making my way to the ground, which is a short walk from our dock. I've entered the Queen's Park Stadium. We have good seats and Australia is batting.

Shane Bond is missing with a gastric problem so the New Zealand attack is vulnerable. James Franklin—who has either been their best or their most expensive bowler in a number of games—will be seen as a weak link by the Australians. They will look to attack him. Gilchrist does, the second ball he faces, and slashes one to deep third man and is caught. Hayden, though, has carnage on his mind. He's racing along. He's charging every bowler, notably Michael Mason and Franklin. Skipper Stephen Fleming is desperate and has to bring on the off-spinner Jetan Patel. It works to a certain extent but fours are spearing off the Hayden bat. It's amazing that although Hayden walks at the bowler when he decides that it's time to make contact, he is deadly still—his head is on a stick, his swing is full and through the line.

Punter Ponting has joined him and he, too, is in the best of form. The ball is flying to the boundary through cover and wide of mid wicket. Punter is a driven man. He wants this World Cup badly. Hayden is bearing down on a half-century, as is Ponting, and they duly pass these milestones almost simultaneously. Ponting's innings is cut short at sixty-six by Patel, and Michael Clarke joins Hayden. He too is soon getting the scoreboard ticking over. How much better a player is Clarke now that he bats more behind his left shoulder? Mick's from the western suburbs but he's now residing on the southern beaches and has a supermodel girlfriend called Lara Bingle. The fact that he's squiring such glamour and driving a Ferrari should not be construed that Mick has changed too much. Did I just write that? Of course he's changed, but he is the front-runner to replace Ponting as Australian captain when the Tasmanian calls it a day after the 2011 World Cup. I wonder if Mick will still have the Ferrari and Lara? He reaches forty-nine and then plays a form of the Irish forward defence shot, allowing a straight ball from Franklin to pitch on middle stump and strike that stump without offering a shot.

Mike Hussey comes in desperately short of match practice and is walking at the ball. Mr Cricket is not hitting many boundaries, but he is running like a hare between the wickets. Hayden has his 100 off 100 balls and then is well caught by Scott Styris whom some believe to be the most unattractive-looking man in world cricket. I'm no oil painting myself, but Scott would get my vote as well. Still he's very good at the bits and pieces, and his effort to run back and take this catch was nothing short of phenomenal.

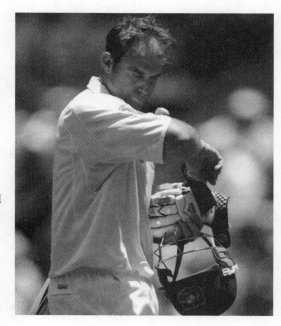

Matthew Hayden created absolute carnage in this game—100 in 100 balls. When he decides to make contact he is deadly still—his head is on a stick, his swing is full and through the line

The overs of the Australian innings are running out. In walks Shane Watson, a much-maligned figure. With just a handful of overs remaining 'Wato' is not always seen as the most ideal player to thrash it from the outset, but immediately he is striking the ball with immense power down the line. He's dealing in boundaries and sixes. Mid-off is cleared, then a huge strike over mid-on, and off the very last ball of the Aussie innings he smites one over cover point for six to reach sixty-five not out. Australia is relatively comfortable at 6–348 from their fifty overs. With Bond absent and Daniel Vettori wicketless from his ten overs (0–60) neither of the New Zealand pivotal men has contributed.

New Zealand is batting. Shaun 'The Wild Thing' Tait is slinging at the speed of light. Fleming is struck on the shoulder and is ruled out caught in the slips.

Meanwhile the Prime Minister of Grenada is at the game and he's doing a tour of the stands. Everybody is cheering and laughing. There's a steel band playing behind him. The whole ground is applauding. This guy is a popular politician. I've never been to an Australian sporting event where John Howard has not been booed. We could learn a lot from these Grenadans about respect for men in office.

Back in the middle Glenn McGrath is being attacked but is picking up regular wickets at the same time. Both Ross Taylor and Styris are gone and Brad Hogg is bemusing these Kiwis with his chinaman. Fair dinkum Ray Charles would have more chance of reading Hogg than these Blackcaps. Hogg finishes with four wickets and it is agreed at the bar at the back of our stand that Hoggy is bowling better than at any stage of his career. Peter Fulton has been the only fellow to withstand the Australian surge so when

Stephen Fleming has such an aristocratic style … He could be the next James Bond when he eventually hangs up the boots

he succumbs to Hogg the Kiwis are all out for 133. Australia has taken an emphatic victory by 215 runs. Their campaign is well on track: unbeaten and winning games very easily.

Although everybody is talking about how long this tournament is, the format suits the Aussies—the defending champions—because they can recover from each match, freshen and build for the upcoming encounter in plenty of time.

I'm walking back to the ship. Grenada is going to fire up tonight as the touring groups party around the many bars of this picturesque little town. I have decided to go back to the ship, have a hot shower, put on my best polo shirt and attack the cocktails.

There are no nip glasses in the Caribbean so when you order a rum punch the barman looks at you and assesses how much of the 'battery acid' you can handle. I've decided to embark on an evening of exotic cocktails. I've drifted into the Martini Bar where I am in the company of Noel and David McKinnon who I met a night or so ago. They're honest, respectful people from Maitland in New South Wales. Noel brought his son David along to share his World Cup adventure. Dave is as kind as a kitten; there wouldn't be a mean bone in his body. The McKinnons are enthusiastic tourists and are having a ball. They're drinking a cocktail from a coconut—it's called Coco Loco. I decide to join them and have a crack at these Coco Locos. There's lots of iced coconut but there's even more Bacardi rum. We get through six each. I'm numb from the hips down but I'm enjoying their company.

Noel played cricket against Doug Walters when Doug was a youngster in Dungog and tells a delightful story of that meeting. He was talking to the opposing captain and was informed that they had a reasonable young player in their team—a thirteen-year-old from Dungog called Kevin (Douglas) Walters.

'Oh yeah, what does he do?' enquired Noel.

'Oh, he's going to bat low, about number eight—he's only very young but he'll open the bowling,' he was told.

'So, he's not a bad bowler?' Noel enquired.

'Oh yeah, he's a very fast bowler, but he can't bat!' Just a little wrong you'd have to say.

Anyway it's near eleven o'clock. I can't walk. I ask Noel and Dave if they can get me a wheelchair. They need one too. We decide to try and make it to our cabins. Half an hour later I'm in cabin 9251 and grateful to be there. I'll sleep well tonight. Australia has won. New Zealand will make the semi-finals nonetheless and I can confidently predict that I have had the last Coco Loco of my career.

Australia v. New Zealand
ICC World Cup 2006–07 (Super 8)

Australia innings		Runs	Balls	Mins	4s	6s
+AC Gilchrist	c Gillespie b Franklin	1	2	7	–	–
ML Hayden	c and b Styris	103	100	150	10	2
*RT Ponting	c Taylor b Patel	66	70	96	7	–
MJ Clarke	b Franklin	49	46	59	7	–
MEK Hussey	c Styris b Franklin	37	44	75	2	–
A Symonds	c Mason b Patel	11	16	20	1	–
SR Watson	not out	65	32	44	4	4
GB Hogg	not out	0	0	3	–	–
NW Bracken	did not bat					
SW Tait	did not bat					
GD McGrath	did not bat					
Extras (1 lb, 10 nb, 5 w)		16				
Total (6 wickets, innings closed, 230 minutes, 50 overs)		348				

Fall of wickets: 1–7 (Gilchrist, 1.1 ov), 2–144 (Ponting, 22.6 ov), 3–216 (Hayden, 32.4 ov), 4–233 (Clarke, 35.3 ov), 5–257 (Symonds, 40.1 ov), 6–334 (Hussey, 49.3 ov)

New Zealand bowling	Overs	Mdns	Runs	Wkts	Wides	No-Balls
Mason	3	0	27	0	1	1
Franklin	8	0	74	3	1	5
Patel	10	0	48	2	–	1
Vettori	10	0	60	0	–	2
Styris	10	0	50	1	2	–
Gillespie	6	0	67	0	–	1
McMillan	3	0	21	0	–	–

New Zealand innings		Runs	Balls	Mins	4s	6s
PG Fulton	b Hogg	62	72	127	5	–
*SP Fleming	c Ponting b Tait	12	9	18	1	1
RL Taylor	c Hussey b McGrath	3	6	8	–	–
SB Styris	c Hayden b McGrath	27	22	30	5	–
CD McMillan	lbw b Tait	1	5	6	–	–
JEC Franklin	b Watson	6	9	11	–	–
+BB McCullum	c Hussey b Hogg	7	16	19	–	–
DL Vettori	c Symonds b Hogg	4	4	7	1	–
MR Gillespie	c McGrath b Hogg	2	8	9	–	–
MJ Mason	c Gilchrist b Tait	0	5	6	–	–
JS Patel	not out	0	1	3	–	–
Extras (2 nb, 7 w)		9				
Total (all out, 127 minutes, 25.5 overs)		133				

Fall of wickets: 1–21 (Fleming, 3.3 ov), 2–29 (Taylor, 5.1 ov), 3–77 (Styris, 11.1 ov), 4–80 (McMillan, 12.3 ov), 5–89 (Franklin, 14.3 ov), 6–111 (McCullum, 19.3 ov), 7–117 (Vettori, 21.1 ov), 8–127 (Gillespie, 23.5 ov), 9–133 (Mason, 24.5 ov), 10–133 (Fulton, 25.5 ov)

Australia bowling	Overs	Mdns	Runs	Wkts	Wides	No-Balls
Bracken	4	0	27	0	1	–
Tait	6	0	32	3	4	1
McGrath	4	0	25	2	–	1
Hogg	6.5	1	29	4	1	–
Watson	5	0	20	1	1	–

Source: Courtesy of cricketarchive.com

SUNDAY, 22 APRIL 2007

MERV HUGHES—
A GOOD BLOKE!

It's another glorious morning in the Caribbean and the good ship *Galaxy* is at full throttle having left Barbados bound for Tortola in the British Virgin Islands.

I've decided to have a healthy morning and a health-compromising afternoon: before midday will be spent soaking up the sun, walking around the boat and having a swim; in the late afternoon sun I'll be enjoying the company of my fellow tourists at the poolside bar.

The last time I was on a ship for this length of time I was bound for Southampton in 1971 to begin a season of county cricket with Somerset. On that occasion I was on board the SS *Australis*, a Greek-owned ship that appeared to have not many more trips in her. We sailed via South America and the Panama Canal and I was in a cabin lower than the one afforded Leonardo DiCaprio in *Titanic*. I shared this tiny underwater telephone box with an alcoholic European and a Russian priest. It was the luck of the draw and not how I'd imagined to be spending four weeks on the high seas.

This time, however, I had a cabin all to myself. Next door is Merv Hughes, a bear of a man whose every footstep inside his room is audible to the whole of the floor. I have a great affection for Merv, always have. He's blessed with a certain degree of insensitivity to all that is going on around him, which has served him well over the years. When he debuted for Australia all those years ago he was much criticised initially, but he shrugged it off and managed to fashion an outstanding career in the baggy green. These days I occasionally pit my aging skills against him in charity matches. He's never bowled anything to me during these games other than a half volley. In the last three matches where I've bowled to him he's hit me 120 yards over deep mid wicket

I have great affection for Merv Hughes, a bear of a man

for six on three separate occasions. I'm not bowling him a wrong
'un ever again. After the third time he'd hit me for a towering
maximum, when he got to the non-striker's end I said, 'Did you
pick the wrong 'un?'

He said, 'Was that the wrong 'un?'. Heh, heh, heh! I love his
off-the-cuff comments.

I started this day at 106 kilograms. I'm going to spend a lot
of it with Merv, so I could end up considerably heavier than
that. It's mid-morning and we're in the Oasis Café on Deck 11.
Merv's having cereal and follows it with bacon and eggs and a
black coffee, no sugar. I have an omelette, french toast, muffin,
two coffees, and a grapefruit just to make me feel good at the
end. I need to be more disciplined at breakfast but it sets me up
for the day.

Merv's from Werribee in Victoria. He once said that, having
toured the world, his favourite hotel anywhere in the hemisphere
was the Racecourse Hotel at Werribee because they do a great
counter lunch. I think that says it all when you've stayed at the
best in the United States and England. He supports the Western
Bulldogs and is unswerving in his passion for that AFL club. He's
also a disciple of the health guru Dr John Tickell and was on
Celebrity Overhaul with the good doctor. His overview these days
appears to be if you work out for an hour and get up a good
sweat you can eat four kilograms of food and it won't affect you. I
can't agree but keep my thoughts to myself. I love Merv's
philosophies on life, and all who played with this funster
thoroughly enjoyed the experience. He has a few rules by which
he now lives. One of them is 'dbo', which is the shortened form
of 'drink beer only'. I'm with him there. I'm not a wine drinker

and I've never been good at it. In fact, wine appreciation is overrated. My wife, on the other hand, is a good wine drinker, she's moderate and she loves a red with her meal and will have a white occasionally. Another of his other tenets is 'nff' 'no friggin' freebies'. I think he's served his time speaking at functions where he gets no return; he's done a lot of charity work over the years. He wants to abolish the dole and do away with university fees. He thinks Australia would be a better place with those two gone. Another of his musings is to introduce capital punishment, and he wants public floggings at the Melbourne Cricket Ground on a Sunday for lesser crimes. Victorians will turn up to anything! They'd flock to this sort of sport, he reckons. He's a bit of an entrepreneur, old Merv. He doesn't like the media or the term 'celebrity' and he thinks Ray Bright is a card. I like Brighty, but I don't see him in the same way.

It's near lunchtime and I've been sunning myself on the back deck of the ship. Merv's been doing laps of the pool area, walking at pace. He's got a sweat up. It's time for lunch. He has two curries, I have one. He said he deserved two after the work he had put in.

It's back to the room for a little 'nanna nap'. Today's been good hanging out with my co-host. We arrange to meet at five o'clock for a couple of beers. We're at the poolside bar, we're hoeing into a few frosties and they're going down a treat. Merv announces he's hungry. It's time for dinner: back to the Oasis Café where it's smorgasbord as always. Merv's having the lamb and the beef and the chicken. I just have the beef and a salad. I've got some notes to make on the semi-finalists so it's back to my room after dinner. Merv says he's going to kick on.

At midnight there's a knock on the door. I've been asleep for an hour or so. It's Merv. He's got pizza from the twenty-four-hour pizza bar on the eleventh floor. He raids my mini bar. We're drinking Heineken. He goes back for more pizza. He's such a good room-mate. He brings me a couple of slices as well. I love pepperoni. It's one o'clock in the morning and we're eating pizza and drinking Heineken in bed. At least I'm in bed. I must weigh 109 kilograms. The mini bar is drained. Merv thinks I've put on weight and says he'll put in a word for me to do *Celebrity Overhaul*. Thanks mate, that's what co-hosts are for.

I fall into a deep sleep surrounded by pepperoni crumbs and empty bottles of Heineken, but my pillow is soft! It's been a long day.

ANZAC DAY …
WE'RE READY!

It's Anzac Day and I'm on board the good ship *Galaxy* having reached the island of St Lucia. We're docked just off the coast and there are 750 Australians waiting to go on to land. We can see the hills of St Lucia in the distance. They know we're coming, they just don't know how many of us there are. The South Africans lie in wait. They are opponents I think we can handle. They're not as tough as Turks.

At 6 am there is a ceremony on board the ship to commemorate Anzac Day. It's quite moving. There are Vietnam veterans in the audience, Dennis Smith from Melbourne is one. He has a tear in his eye. Apparently he lost friends from his battalion during that war. Eighty-six-year-old Ray Kyatt makes a brief speech about what it means to be an Anzac. He lauds the United States and says we owe them a lot. He's very pro-American and feels we are in their debt after what they did for us during the wars. It is a sentiment shared by many. My father was a POW in Changi. He didn't speak much about his treatment at the hands of the Japanese but he was deeply scarred. I saw photos taken before his imprisonment and then those taken after peace was declared. They showed two different people. My old man never quite recovered. I loved him dearly.

Today is match day. Australia plays the Proteas in the second semi-final. New Zealand was valiant but did not possess enough game breakers to undo Sri Lanka in the first semi-final yesterday. Sri Lankan captain Mahela Jayawardene played one of the all-time great World Cup innings and was justifiably man of the match. He has the face of a choirboy but the bat swing of an executioner. With impact players like Lasith Malinga and Muttiah

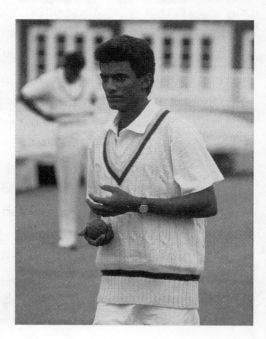

Muttiah Muralitharan was a stunning omission from the Sri Lankan attack in the first semi-final of the World Cup

Jacques Kallis—there were rumours of dissent in the South African camp over the brilliant all-rounder's scoring rate in one-day cricket

Muralitharan in the Sri Lankan line-up they are going to be a real handful in the final. Australia has to get past a South African team which is rumoured to have not enjoyed the happiest of camps throughout this long World Cup. There have been reports of excessive drinking and wives who have not got on as famously as they might have. There are reports too that Jacques Kallis and Graeme Smith have not seen eye to eye on team tactics. Further to the South African dilemma is that Makhaya Ntini has lost form and will not play in the final. Andre Nel has made the XI despite a broken finger.

After the dawn service I'm having breakfast with Paul and Robert Strutt, brothers who are enjoing the trip. Both are cricket enthusiasts. One of them went to Cranbrook School in Sydney but appears normal. I have had numerous discussions with the

Strutts over the last few days. They are the most genuine of cricket followers—it's demeaning to call them 'tragics'. These boys just love the game with a passion. Chris and Di Hoskins, a delightful couple from Adelaide, are breakfasting at the next table. I shared a few beers with Chris the previous evening. Generally I've never enjoyed good relationships with South Australians, but the Hoskins are proof that I can get on with people from the city of churches—ours is a groundbreaking relationship.

It's time to go to the ground. St Lucia is rich in natural beauty. Water sports dominate the attractions and they have splendid beaches, warm sea and heat all year round. There aren't too many roads in and out of Beausejour Stadium and consequently there are huge traffic jams on match day. We have seats valued at $126.00 each. My touring group expects them to be premium and offer cover. They're neither! We are in a stand of the three Ts—timber, tin and temporary! It's already thirty degrees Celsius and this stand has the potential to be a sauna by mid-afternoon. Still, it's a World Cup semi-final and we're ringside.

Smith has won the toss and decides to bat. The St Lucia pitch has yielded runs in every game and it has been no disadvantage to bat second. Determined not to allow Nathan Bracken to settle down, Smith runs at the left-hander and is defeated by an outswinger that hits his off stump in the second over. Kallis, too, plays an out-of-character shot when he tries to squirt a Glenn McGrath yorker through point, presenting only a quarter of the bat face and losing middle and off stump for five.

With their two best players gone Australia is all over the South Africans. De Villiers falls victim to a Tait flier and Prince plays extravagantly at McGrath and edges to Gilchrist. Boucher is out first ball nicking to first slip. At 5–27 Herschelle Gibbs gets a thick inside edge off Tait and inexplicably is given not out. A score line of 6–27 perhaps would have had us back on board the *Galaxy* by mid-afternoon.

Justin Kemp, however, though seen as fragile against the short ball, comes in and plays an innings of some substance. Brad Hogg bowls and returns 1–24 from ten overs to further emphasise his development as a wrist spinner of some significance. This is a day where anything wayward from the chinaman bowler may mean momentum shifting back to the Proteas, but Hogg's control and skilful variation are irresistible.

Brad Hogg, the uncomplicated spinner from the West, has attracted a stand banner, complete with goofy face and protruding tongue

Winners are grinners...champion bowler Glenn McGrath may have been winding down, but no-one collared him in the World Cup. For good measure he snaffled a wicket with his last ball in international cricket

'Hoggy' fashioned his skills all those years ago with lonely 6 am bowling sessions in the dead of winter at the WACA indoor cricket centre. Hogg apparently had a key and used to let himself in for his one-man training sessions. Word has it that State coaching staff eventually changed the centre's locks to avoid him burning himself out.

All the other Australian guns fired. McGrath has 3–18 from eight overs, Tait has four wickets and Bracken is as miserly as ever. When Shane Watson bowls Carl Langeveldt it's all over at 149.

The pitch has settled down. There's still a little bit of sideways movement but Australia should get this easily.

My fellow tourists are falling like flies—the heat is relentless— a few are going back to the boat, others are seeking refuge under the covered stands. I'm with Ian from central Queensland and his wife. They're tough country stock. Despite the debilitating temperature his stoic wife is by his side in jeans gritting her teeth. He asks her to get him a drink and she says, 'You've got two legs!' and pulls her bucket hat tighter over her head. Gilchrist is bowled immediately by Langeveldt and at 1–1 people are starting to think this could be an uneasy chase.

In comes Ricky Ponting the captain and he's away immediately. Five boundaries fly off the captain's bat. Hayden is looking more circumspect. Ponting tries something a little too extravagant against Nel and loses off stump. Nel appears to be someone whom his team-mates adore but who alienates opponents and their supporters. Batsmen get out to him because they're looking to hammer him into the next postcode.

At number four Michael Clarke is under some pressure. He's been one of the stars of the tournament and straight away looks in good touch. Hayden has a slash down the ground at Pollock and is taken well by Smith at mid-off.

Andrew Symonds comes in. He doesn't mess around in these circumstances and is clubbing the ball like a blacksmith. Clarke has laid the ground work with some terrific strokes through mid wicket and extra cover, and Symonds hits three quick fours to get Australia home in the thirty-second over. The Aussies have flogged the Proteas by seven wickets and our group is ecstatic as we head back to the *Galaxy*. Of course sunburn and dehydration are a factor, but a shower and a few frosties will right all that.

Back on the ship we're celebrating. Clive Lloyd joins me at the poolside bar. No, it's not *the* Clive Lloyd, it's Clive 'Polly'

Lloyd from Airlie Beach, Queensland. Polly is a tremendous fellow, a former cook with the Navy who likes fishing and telling yarns. He tells me his story on the second night of our cruise. When his marriage broke up and left him virtually bankrupt he moved to North Queensland and bought a cab. Mortgaged to the hilt and approaching his mid-fifties it didn't look good for old 'Polly'. Then God intervened. He and nine other cabbies won $6 million in Lotto. Suddenly Clive was secure and he intended to enjoy that state of mind. He is travelling the world, laughing and having the occasional drink. He loved a drink in his prime but for health reasons he only has the odd tipple these days. Clive confided that over the decades he's been reasonably popular with the opposite sex. I asked him his secret. He said, 'It's my opening line.'

'What is it?' I ask.

Polly enthused, 'I simply walk up to them offer my hand and say, 'Hi, I'm Clive. What do you think of me so far?'

Today has been draining. I take my leave from my party who are celebrating qualification for the final in real style. I'm hungry and stop off at the all-night pizza outlet on the eleventh floor. I need a 'traveller'; there are two sets of stairs to my room and two slices of pepperoni should see me there—responsible eating has gone out the porthole on this cruise.

Australia has triumphed on Anzac Day. It's been memorable for any number of reasons. Murali and company await the final. That's going to be quite a day in Bridgetown.

Australia v. South Africa
ICC World Cup 2006–07 (Semi-final)

South Africa innings		Runs	Balls	Mins	4s	6s
*GC Smith	b Bracken	2	5	10	–	–
AB de Villiers	c Gilchrist b Tait	15	34	39	3	–
JH Kallis	b McGrath	5	9	12	1	–
HH Gibbs	c Gilchrist b Tait	39	49	77	6	–
AG Prince	c Gilchrist b McGrath	0	2	4	–	–
+MV Boucher	c Hayden b McGrath	0	1	1	–	–
JM Kemp	not out	49	91	151	4	1
AJ Hall	c Gilchrist b Tait	3	8	14	–	–
SM Pollock	c and b Hogg	5	13	15	1	–
A Nel	c Clarke b Tait	8	41	45	1	–
CK Langeveldt	b Watson	6	10	18	1	–
Extras (4 lb, 13 w)		17				
Total (all out, 199 minutes, 43.5 overs)		149				

Fall of wickets: 1–7 (Smith, 2.3 ov), 2–12 (Kallis, 5.3 ov), 3–26 (de Villiers, 8.5 ov), 4–27 (Prince, 9.4 ov), 5–27 (Boucher, 9.5 ov), 6–87 (Gibbs, 22.5 ov), 7–93 (Hall, 26.1 ov), 8–103 (Pollock, 29.4 ov), 9–130 (Nel, 40.1 ov), 10–149 (Langeveldt, 43.5 ov)

Australia bowling	Overs	Mdns	Runs	Wkts	Wides	No-Balls
Bracken	7	2	15	1	–	–
McGrath	8	1	18	3	1	–
Tait	10	0	39	4	5	–
Watson	8.5	0	49	1	–	–
Hogg	10	2	24	1	3	–

Australia innings		Runs	Balls	Mins	4s	6s
+AC Gilchrist	b Langeveldt	1	5	4	–	–
ML Hayden	c Smith b Pollock	41	60	115	4	–
*RT Ponting	b Nel	22	25	38	5	–
MJ Clarke	not out	60	86	109	8	–
A Symonds	not out	18	16	29	3	–
MEK Hussey	did not bat					
SR Watson	did not bat					
GB Hogg	did not bat					
NW Bracken	did not bat					
SW Tait	did not bat					
GD McGrath	did not bat					
Extras (5 lb, 3 nb, 3 w)		11				
Total (3 wickets, 146 minutes, 31.3 overs)		153				

Fall of wickets: 1–1 (Gilchrist, 1.1 ov), 2–44 (Ponting, 8.6 ov), 3–110 (Hayden, 24.4 ov)

South Africa bowling	Overs	Mdns	Runs	Wkts	Wides	No-Balls
Pollock	5	1	16	1	–	–
Langeveldt	6	0	34	1	1	1
Kallis	5	1	20	0	1	1
Nel	7	1	31	1	1	–
Hall	6.3	0	43	0	–	1
Kemp	2	0	4	0	–	–

Source: Courtesy of cricketarchive.com

THE WORLD CUP FINAL, RINGSIDE!

The *Galaxy* has cruised into Barbados overnight. The Kensington Oval will host the final between Australia and Sri Lanka. The 2007 World Cup culminates today at the finest ground in the Caribbean and I'll be there with my touring party. The atmosphere at any World Cup final is always gripping. Seven long weeks of competition and it's down to two. Australia is a justifiable favourite—it has easily won every match in this competition. Sri Lanka has a number of match winners but may not have the bowling depth against this vibrant Aussie outfit. Ricky Ponting has said that if this had been a World Cup soccer campaign, we would have won every game 4–0—and we intend to win the final by a similar margin.

I'm on board breakfasting with the John and Catherine Cherry. They're a charming couple from Pelican Point, Queensland, who met in fifth grade at school and are still together five decades later. They are true cricket people, though according to customs officials John may just have a darker side. At every security check so far the couple have been pulled aside because of their surname. There must have been a Mafia don called John Cherry because this understated Australian has attracted unbelievable scrutiny every time his passport is presented.

I'm through customs without too many problems. I'm joined on the walk to the ground by Gary Lloyd and Bill Hoffman, interesting cricket people from Jamestown, South Australia, who say they are enjoying the trip tremendously. Gary has suffered poor health in recent times but is reputed to have been one of the best country cricketers in his state, and Bill is a knockabout fellow with strong views on the game. Halfway to the ground we're alongside Geoff McCormack. He's from Melbourne and on tour with his son Martin. Geoff has the demeanour of a man who has done well in business and is more than a little involved in thoroughbred racing. He too is looking forward to the day.

I'm in a queue outside the Kensington Oval. It's changed a lot since I was last here in 1979 with the World Series cricket Australians. On that day I made an ill-fated decision to embark on a road run back to the hotel. It ended when a woman drove her car through a stop sign at an intersection and struck me, breaking my leg in three places and straining my medial ligaments. The collision effectively ended my career. When we passed the intersection on the way from the dock I suddenly felt a sharp pain my leg—I'll never forget that cross street!

Inside the oval I'm immediately taken aback at how much it has changed. The new stands are cream and white and look fresh. The temporary stand is subtle. The house full sign has gone up.

We have good seats, we're in a covered stand, and our numbers have swelled dramatically. There are a few other touring parties in our stand. Carl Rackemann—dear old 'Mocka'—is here with twenty from his home state, and it's always good to chat with this mild-mannered former Queensland fast bowler.

Australia will go into this vital match with the same side that has torn apart most teams in the competition, while Sri Lanka has preferred Dilhara Fernando to Farveez Maharoof. This could be a mistake as Fernando gets people out but leaks copious runs in between times. The Australian tactic will be to attack him from the outset.

There was a drizzle while we were walking to the ground and it has increased. Clouds have come over Bridgetown and the start of play has been delayed. The rain has got heavier. I'm starting to wonder whether we'll get any play at all, but then, in a twinkling, it lifts. Time has been eaten away and a ground announcement says that the match will be a thirty-eight-overs-a-side contest. I look at my watch and do quick calculations. The game is going to finish in the dark. The light goes at around 5.45 pm—this match will finish at 6.10–6.15 pm. There is no twilight in the Caribbean. The sun sets and you go from being able to see to darkness in a heartbeat. This could be trouble.

Gilchrist and Hayden burst out of the dressing-rooms and Chaminda Vaas is on his way for the first ball of this final. Can Gilchrist lift his way out of a form slump? Hayden is the most prolific batsman of the tournament but Gilchrist has so far failed to play an innings of any significance. Unbeknown to anybody, 'Gilly' is batting with a squash ball in his glove. His coach, Bob Meuleman, a delicate batsman for Western Australia, who worked the ball nicely to third man for a number of years, has suggested that by placing a squash ball in his bottom hand batting glove the pressure on the bat will be eased, allowing his top hand to control the bat face more and reduce the chances of sliced drives to point. The ploy seems to be working. Gilchrist is playing the innings of his life. Well, he's played a number of them, but this arguably could be the best innings ever in a World Cup final. After an over of assessing whether Vaas is swinging the ball, Gilly has decided that there's no movement through the air and has decided to take to the air himself. Sixes are landing in the terraces. The slinger Malinga has been one of the Sri Lankan trumps throughout the preliminary games. He bowls a maiden over and supporters of the underdog throughout the ground applaud respectfully.

Young fast bowling guns with interesting actions—Shaun Tait and Lasith Malinga

I'm sitting in front of three Barbadians: Bernard and his wife, Olivia, and her sister. They look good cricket folk. They're bemused by the fact that this bald, slightly overweight veteran seated near them is signing autographs and posing regularly for photos. Bernard asks me if I had played. I explain that I came here in 1973 with Ian Chappell's Australians. When I formally introduce myself his face lights up, but given that I went wicketless against Barbados, and in the Test match a week later at this ground, he doesn't talk me through my Bridgetown triumphs. I notice, too, he's not cheering Gilchrist's onslaught and when Malinga bowls another tight over, he shouts 'Bowled Malinga'. I half turn my head, raising an eyebrow. He creases up with laughter. Bernard's a regular guy but it is clear to me now that a number of the locals have decided to support Sri Lanka. With so many Australian touring parties inside the ground you could almost be forgiven for thinking Australia is playing at home.

Gilchrist is unstoppable. He's ripping over mid wicket, he's slicing over cover and the sixes are raining into the stands. Each time he picks up the bat with intent, people rise from their seats in expectation and cheer the ball as it sails into the bleachers.

Malinga picks out Hayden for thirty-eight and Ponting strides to the wicket to play a somewhat circumspect innings. The captain strikes just one boundary and one six in making thirty-seven. Gilchrist, however, has put the Sri Lankans to the sword. He's eventually out for 149 from 104 balls with eight scintillating sixes and thirteen boundaries. Seldom has there been such carnage in a major one-day final. Fellow tourists were musing at one point that he may get 200. It didn't look out of the question when he put his foot down after reaching 100.

Andrew Symonds and Michael Clarke applied some icing to the cake and after thirty-eight overs the tournament favourites have reached 4–281. Fernando had gone for seventy-four runs in eight overs and both Murali and Vaas failed to take a wicket in conceding almost seven runs an over. Word reached us later that coach John Buchanan told his team that they had to play 'the power game' when the match had been reduced by twelve overs.

After a shortened break the Sri Lankan openers are taking guard. Upul Tharanga and Sanath Jayasuriya must get their team away to a flyer. The computer will have told Buchanan and company that left-arm quick men have had success against these Sri Lankan openers in the past, and in the third over Bracken draws an edge from Tharanga and it's 1–7.

Sangakkara, a world-class player, enters at number three. The underdogs are running out of time. The required run rate is high but the Australians are conceding regular boundaries and the men from Colombo are still in the game. Shaun Tait is quick but expensive and going at seven runs an over. Glenn McGrath is difficult to attack but every team in this competition so far has made attempts at mauling the aging veteran. Today is no different. Shane Watson is not moving the ball off the pitch or through the air, and both Jayasuriya and Sangakkara are working him past square leg and through the covers for runs. Brad Hogg has been held back but when he's introduced he concedes nineteen runs in just three overs. These left-handers are able to get under Hogg, and Ponting decides that he needs a slower bowler who may make the ball stay down. He turns to Michael Clarke—his round arm spinners slide more than bounce on particular surfaces and straight away Jayasuriya is down the pitch and missing a gasunder. This was a pivotal wicket. Sangakkara had gone previously to Hogg holing out to Punter in the covers.

The light is fading. There is further delay. The match is shortened to thirty-six overs. At the thirty-third over mark and with the Sri Lankans well behind on the Duckworth Lewis method, the umpires agree that it is too dark and that the match is over.

The Australian players immediately launch into their love-in. They have won their third World Cup in a row. Emotions pour out. Players are kissing, hugging, embracing. The Australian supporters are going nuts in the stands. We've come for this and the players have delivered. Okay, there's a lot of pride in this victory, but the small matter of $US300,000 prize money may have contributed a little to the excitement. For Brad Haddin and Mitchell Johnson, who had not played a game, this was a 'fat day'. No wonder they were running the drinks out with great alacrity at every opportunity.

Hang on, hold your horses, Rudi Koertzen has emerged from the darkness gesturing. He's insisting after consultation with match referee Jeff Crowe, that the final three overs have to be bowled tonight to complete the match, otherwise we're all back tomorrow for the anticlimax. McGrath has taken a wicket with his last ball of international cricket, and after Ponting agrees that they will bowl out the overs he guarantees that only spinners will be used. So he brings on his best bowler in the dark, Andrew Symonds. Malinga is stumped; nobody could see the ball or the batting crease but he walks off anyway. Fernando comes in and blocks six balls and it's all over officially.

There's another love-in. The ground is in darkness, lights are poor at the Kensington Oval at any time. There is a girl singing in

Glenn McGrath with his final prize—the World Cup. Australia will miss him more than Warney

the middle of the ground dressed in black. Nobody can see her but she has a good voice. She's part of the after-match ceremony. The microphone levels are poor. Nobody in the stands can hear the official speeches. Who cares? We've won the cup. I'm back to the poolside bar to celebrate. I'm bolting through the streets of Barbados to the *Galaxy*. I stop at every stop sign nonetheless. You can't be too careful around these parts!

I'm safely back on board the *Galaxy* and the Whitehouses from Blackwater, Queensland, come and join me for a celebratory drink. They're good people, Tom and his wife, Jenny. The Whitehouses are in mining and Tom was originally from Wynyard, Tasmania, but couldn't be happier with his life in the sunshine state. He and Jenny are in a business where they are working 24–7. He gets up at 5 am every day, seven days a week and goes to bed at 10 pm.

They're as Aussie as and both like a drink. Clint, their son, and his attractive wife, Bianca, are with them. Clint convinced Tom and Jenny that they needed to come on the holiday to get away and they've had a ball. Clint may be from outback Queensland, but he's been around the world as a backpacker and he has a world-street wisdom about him. Bianca is from a neighbouring town. Tom thought that Clint would marry a girl that he met on one of his many overseas jaunts, but he eventually married somebody who lived only a few kilometres away. They're happy. Tom, Jenny, Clint and Bianca Whitehouse are the ideal tourists. After a couple of beers with them I'm tired. It's been a long day. We were up early to get clearance through customs. I'm in my room around midnight. Merv bursts through the door carrying pepperoni and Heinekens. We demolish his goodies and I fall into the sleep of a winner. We've won the Cup!

Australia v. Sri Lanka
ICC World Cup 2006–07 (Final)

Australia innings		Runs	Balls	Mins	4s	6s
+AC Gilchrist	c Silva b Fernando	149	104	129	13	8
ML Hayden	c Jayawardene b Malinga	38	55	100	3	1
*RT Ponting	run out (Jayawardene)	37	42	53	1	1
A Symonds	not out	23	21	39	2	–
SR Watson	b Malinga	3	3	3	–	–
MJ Clarke	not out	8	6	10	1	–
MEK Hussey	did not bat					
GB Hogg	did not bat					
NW Bracken	did not bat					
SW Tait	did not bat					
GD McGrath	did not bat					
Extras (4 lb, 3 nb, 16 w)		23				
Total (4 wickets, innings closed,						
169 minutes, 38 overs)		281				

Fall of wickets: 1–172 (Hayden, 22.5 ov), 2–224 (Gilchrist, 30.3 ov), 3–261 (Ponting, 35.4 ov), 4–266 (Watson, 36.2 ov)

Sri Lanka bowling	Overs	Mdns	Runs	Wkts	Wides	No-Balls
Vaas	8	0	54	0	1	2
Malinga	8	1	49	2	–	–
Fernando	8	0	74	1	4	1
Muralitharan	7	0	44	0	2	–
Dilshan	2	0	23	0	1	–
Jayasuriya	5	0	33	0	–	–

Sri Lanka innings		Runs	Balls	Mins	4s	6s
WU Tharanga	c Gilchrist b Bracken	6	8	11	1	–
ST Jayasuriya	b Clarke	63	67	108	9	–
+KC Sangakkara	c Ponting b Hogg	54	52	82	6	1
*DPMD Jayawardene	lbw b Watson	19	19	32	1	–
LPC Silva	b Clarke	21	22	42	1	1
TM Dilshan	run out (Clarke->McGrath)	14	13	20	2	–
RP Arnold	c Gilchrist b McGrath	1	2	9	–	–
WPUJC Vaas	not out	11	21		–	–
SL Malinga	st Gilchrist b Symonds	10	6		–	1
CRD Fernando	not out	1	6		–	–
M Muralitharan	did not bat					
Extras (1 lb, 14 w)		15				
Total (8 wickets, innings closed, 36 overs)		215				

Fall of wickets: 1–7 (Tharanga, 2.1 ov), 2–123 (Sangakkara, 19.5 ov), 3–145 (Jayasuriya, 22.6 ov), 4–156 (Jayawardene, 25.5 ov), 5–188 (Dilshan, 29.6 ov), 6–190 (Silva, 30.1 ov), 7–194 (Arnold, 31.5 ov), 8–211 (Malinga, 33.6 ov)

Australia bowling	Overs	Mdns	Runs	Wkts	Wides	No-Balls
Bracken	6	1	34	1	1	–
Tait	6	0	42	0	2	–
McGrath	7	0	31	1	1	–
Watson	7	0	49	1	3	–
Hogg	3	0	19	1	–	–
Clarke	5	0	33	2	2	–
Symonds	2	0	6	1	–	–

Source: Courtesy of cricketarchive. com

TWO PARAGRAPHS— NOT NEARLY ENOUGH

I'm sitting having breakfast, as I always do, at my desk. I've got a banana, sourdough bread with honey and a short black espresso. I don't know whether it's the ideal breakfast but I just can't handle cereal. My wife is losing kilos seemingly every hour. She's so disciplined—and she's turned into a gym junkie. Still, I'm comfortable with what I'm eating.

I'm perusing the *Daily Telegraph*. Sure it's a tabloid but it covers so much of what I'm interested in. I don't read the back or front page. Perhaps that's why I feel the publication has credibility. There is a death notice in the Sports Section today informing readers that Bernie Hall, a veteran boxing trainer, has passed away aged seventy-nine. Bernie has received four paragraphs. That's pretty good. I met him in the 1970s and enjoyed his company one evening over a few beers. He is a former pug who then took to training and was a pretty feisty character: he once jumped into the ring after a fight to throw a few himself. The fact that he managed four paragraphs about his life was something. The *Sydney Sun* afforded me just two paragraphs when I retired from first-class cricket; yet I'd played twenty-four Tests for Australia and made over seventy appearances for New South Wales. It's not ego, I just felt my whole career deserved more than two miserly paragraphs. I'd love to get more than two paragraphs when I pass away. It's almost an ambition now that when I go I don't want to read: 'Kerry O'Keeffe has died aged ... O'Keeffe played twenty-four Tests for Australia and was an ABC cricket commentator between 2001 and 2007.' Surely somebody could come up with a few more words, even if they're critical. Some very great men have probably got only two paragraphs on their passing, but I feel that at fifty-seven I've done enough and made enough of an impression on people for my death to generate more than a handful of lines.

It seems unfair to me that some people have led extraordinarily interesting and committed lives and achieved so much and yet are dismissed so summarily when they pass. I wouldn't mind a section in every paper where somebody who merits more than a couple of paragraphs gets their life encapsulated in say eight to ten paragraphs. Two 'pars' just simply informs the reader that you lived and that you've died.

I reckon I've only really contributed substantially to those around me in the last ten years. I don't know about an epitaph but I do want to be remembered for the fact that my wife and I raised our children as well as we could have and that I've made some people laugh. These are accomplishments that should not go unrecognised. Every parent who successfully raises children past adolescence should generate at least two paragraphs.

Underworld figures get double-page spreads in newspapers when they leave this earth. It's not a gripe, it's just that every day I wake up now I'm thinking of Mohammed Ali who said, 'When I go to bed tonight I want to have had the best day I could and have done something for somebody during that day'. If I can go to bed twelve or so hours later I reckon I can accumulate enough good to produce half a dozen paragraphs at least. Okay, that's my whinge. It's over. I might have another short black. But when I pass away, I want more than two paragraphs—even if they're full of sledges!

SUNDAY, 13 MAY 2007

DR CYRIL LATIMER— THE SLOWEST FAST BOWLER EVER

It hasn't been the best of weeks. For some reason the travel associated with my guest speaking has worn me down and the nervousness which grips me before each engagement has taken a toll.

It's a bright autumn day in Sydney and I've found the attraction of Centennial Park in this sort of weather hard to resist over the years. I've known Dr Cyril Latimer for almost thirty years. He's been a tremendous confidant during that period. I've appreciated his counsel on a number of occasions. As he lives in Randwick I've given him a ring and arranged to walk a full lap of the park. Cyril and I played cricket together for the Sydney University Veterans in the mid to late '80s. He is the slowest opening bowler the game has ever seen and possibly the worst batsman. His only stroke of any consequence was a sweep which he played to every single delivery. During his illustrious career with the Vets the highest Cyril averaged with the bat was 4.0, but it was his work with the new ball that commanded attention. Opponents could not restrain themselves from trying to hit him out of the park, but his worth to our side, despite an economy rate of seven or eight runs per over, was that he got batsmen out. As Jim Maxwell might say, 'So many drowned in honey'.

Cyril and I have been walking around Centennial Park on and off for twenty years. His wife, Helen, is desperately ill with a brain tumour. Dr Helen Beh is tremendously popular, a great mind and a fighter. Her doctors have said only three in 1000 beat the kind of tumour she has. I'm tipping her to be one of the three.

As Cyril and I walk we reminisce about our time together with the Vets. I loved City and Suburban cricket. I treated each match

Cyril Latimer—a hit to him at mid-on was a guaranteed single! His friendship has been valuable for a long time

as a Test match. Sadly, I wish I had it over again. Even though I never got wickets. I don't know why. The cow shot used to beat me all the time. It was strange to see batsmen initially nervous at the non-striker's end when I first came on to bowl, but who by the time I had completed one or two overs were running their partner out in order to get to the striker's end to face me. But I batted well during my C and S career. I played in the V. All the annual reports talk of how straight I played. I found the pull shot ugly and even though the matches were only thirty-five overs a side I refused to hit across the line, regardless of the situation. It's something inside me that says, no, it's not the right shot despite the fact that quick runs were required. I have a different attitude these days when I play. I try to hit the first ball I face back over the bowler's head for four. I wish I'd had that overview during my career.

Cyril sails these days. He is the captain of a Brolga 33—a thirty-three-footer that he competes in on Sydney Harbour every Saturday. The length of his craft is the absolute limit for acceptance in the Sydney to Hobart classic. He talks this day about his ambition to do a 'Hobart'.

Cyril's story is a lesson to everyone. He arrived here as Able Seaman Latimer in 1962 from Belfast with £10 in his kit—and he went on to become a Professor of Psychology. It's a great story. He lives in a rambling Victorian house in Randwick and he's the mildest of men. Throughout my lean trot in the '80s and '90s, it was always Cyril who spoke positively whenever we walked. He talked of never giving up, of playing to your strengths, of accepting rejection, of not worrying what others thought, of not worrying about downsides. He admired that I would trade futures, that I would bowl leg breaks, that I would stand up in front of 200 people and attempt comedy. He had great admiration that I would take on tasks that others would shy away from and wondered why I would beat myself up if my challenges didn't work out. His friendship has been valuable for a long time and I doubt whether there is anyone prouder outside my family that I'm now enjoying the happiest period of my life.

Cyril was my mid-on throughout most of my career with the Vets. At mid-off was Thos Hodgson, a well-known Sydney barrister. This was not Symonds and Ponting attacking the ball, daring batsmen to attempt a sneaky single; this was a guaranteed run to all who aimed in their direction. Their success rate at taking catches was one in ten. If a catch went towards either of them they'd both call 'Yours Kerry' at the top of their voices. Thos is a cricket enthusiast and a great fellow. He's a family law barrister and throughout the six or seven years of playing cricket with him I never saw him bowl a delivery, take a catch or score a run. He paid his subscription for the day's cricket, batted infrequently at number eleven, was never asked to roll out an over, and was almost anonymous in the field, yet over a cold beer at the end of the day he'd declare how much he'd loved the outing. These men are rare.

Cyril's greatest day came when he was heavy with flu against Old Cranbrookians at Dangar Oval. He took 5–60 off five overs and batsmen were either hitting him into the palaces of Rose Bay or straight up in the air. I snaffled three catches off him at mid wicket. Cyril loved bowling, but he lacked pace and it was said that he was so slow that he could set his field after he'd released the ball. His best performance came in the summer of 1987–88 when he took forty wickets. He has confessed that there was no reason for his golden summer that year. There was no carefully planned pre-season fitness regime, though he did admit that on Friday night he'd reduced his sherry intake by half. What a pro!

As the sun set this afternoon we talked about having a Vets reunion from the mid '80s. It's been over twenty years now. We discussed getting together at the University Club in Phillip Street, Sydney. People like Thos, and David Garnsey, our left-handed wicket-keeper who punched catches to gully but whose knowledge of sport is unparalleled; David Fox, the off spinner who enjoyed his wickets more than he did those of others; Tom Nevell, aged seventy-two, who I ran out on a windy day at Erskineville Oval. As he passed me I shouted 'Tack', forlornly hoping that this chugging vessel could somehow make his ground; Greg Cooney, our left-arm opening bowler who swung it more than Cyril but at about the same pace; the late Dennis Meintjes, a much-loved cricket enthusiast, who sadly died with thirty more years of modest cricket left in him; and Brian Nicholson, a left-arm orthodox spinner who was dapper and civil throughout the most testing of confrontations. We'll have that dinner this summer and it'll be a rollicking affair.

I love Sydney Uni Vets. I follow them every Monday morning these days. They seem to have fallen upon hard times. They don't win very much.

Cyril and I finish the walk and have coffee back at Randwick. Helen is in good spirits. She is a tremendous supporter of ABC Cricket, following Ashes campaigns, World Cups and domestic cricket religiously via the national broadcaster. Her mind is as sharp as ever but the therapy has affected her body. I drive away from the Latimers and say a prayer that Helen can pull through. Her eyes tell me that she has a chance.

FORMER TEAM-MATES ... WHERE ARE THEY NOW?

I had a long conversation with Gary Gilmour on the phone this morning. His new liver is functioning perfectly and his voice is so much more upbeat than it was in the dark hours when his former vital organ was failing. Gary's journey from diseased liver to the replacement was a lesson to everybody to never give up despite the bleakness of the outlook. There is a waiting list for organ transplants and Gary advanced up the list from fifth, to third and then second. And eventually 'Gus' was top of the list. I can only imagine his feelings whenever the phone rang at home, as his life was slipping away. Could it be his 'time' this time?

A couple of months before the operation that saved his life, a fundraiser was held in Newcastle for the former all-rounder. A packed house of nearly 500 people at Wests Newcastle Leagues Club saw firsthand the frailty and the grave situation that confronted the beneficiary. These days Gus is still unable to wheel down twenty overs into the breeze, and is still under heavy medication to prevent organ rejection, but all those who have known him throughout his cricket and private life rejoice in the fact that he's still with us.

I played the majority of my interstate and Test cricket with Gus. He was seen as the next big thing, the next Alan Davidson, when he emerged from Newcastle all those years ago. But in his fifteen Tests he took just fifty-four wickets at an average of 26.03 with his left-arm pace, and averaged twenty-three with the bat. Considering his natural gifts this was seen as underperformance. A gout sufferer throughout his career, Gus played for the enjoyment perhaps more than the accomplishment. His game was different to mine and I envied his skills and attitude. He was aggressive. He didn't fear failure and crowds warmed to the entertainment he provided them.

Gus Gilmour was naturally gifted and played for enjoyment. I envied his skills and attitude

Fearsome speedster Jeff Thomson shows batting skill, nonchalantly playing one away to the onside during his almost match-saving innings against England in Melbourne, 1982

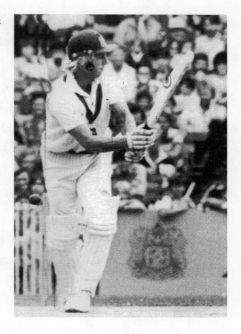

The most memorable innings I can recall him playing for New South Wales was against Queensland at the Gabba in November 1976. Jeff Thomson had taken 7–33 in the first innings to bowl us out for seventy-one, and, following on, was bowling as fast as I've ever seen the ball delivered. The evening before our follow on we'd been up to some high jinks. It was a prolonged session of cocktails and Gus had led the way by embarking on several shouts of Green Lizards, a lethal combination of chartreuse and rum. The following morning nobody felt like batting, especially facing Thommo's balls at 155 kilometres per hour. Nonetheless, Gus went out to bat bareheaded and embarked on an innings of unbelievable power. He finished with 115 off just seventy balls, and kept striking Thomson bouncers into the starting boxes of the greyhound track which encircled the ground at that time.

At the other end I could barely see Thommo, let alone make contact with any of his missiles, and lost middle and off stump for just one. Neither Gus nor I have tried a Green Lizard since.

Despite our different outlooks on how the game should be played, Gus always showed me the utmost respect. He may have taken the micky out of me on a few occasions, but it was never mean spirited, and there was never an undertone of bullying. Along with a majority of his era he signed with World Series Cricket in 1977, and although he's not one to show too much regret he did admit to me a few years later that he would love to have captained Australia, and that the period during World Series Cricket may just have been his opportunity. Many who played with Gus saw him more as a loyal lieutenant than a skipper, and because he kept his thoughts to himself most of the time it would have been difficult to detect leadership ambitions.

Talking to Gus this morning generated a number of thoughts about fellow team-mates with whom I've lost contact. Cricket is a strange game. Although it has all the team fundamentals it's basically a collection of individuals who try for themselves in a team environment. Despite representing the Blues in over seventy matches, I don't really talk to too many players of my era all that much. Lenny 'Slippery' Pascoe is somebody with whom I am in regular contact. Formerly known as Len Durtanovich (I never did find out why he changed his name), the big fast bowler played fourteen Tests and twenty-nine one day internationals in the '70s and '80s. Recently I came close to selecting him in my best limited over team of all time because of his terrific strike rate in that form of the game. Slippery is a sweetheart. I've known him for forty years and he's a very respectful individual. In fact, I've never seen him get angry other than on the cricket field. Off the field he's courteous and gracious to everybody. He spends endless hours listening to Dean Martin CDs—I don't know why, but he's a curious mix, is Slippery. These days he makes a living in the sports entertainment business and boasts that he has the best Elvis Presley imitator in Australia. If Lenny had been more level-headed on the field he may have achieved greater rewards.

I captained New South Wales only once in my career, against Victoria at the Melbourne Cricket Ground in the mid '70s. The Victorians had won the toss and decided to bat and the opening batsman was Les Stillman—a noted hooker and cutter. It was roundly agreed at the team meeting the night before that if there was any movement to be had early with the new ball we should keep it up to Stillman as he was seen as a 'nicker'. Len took the first over from what is now the Great Southern stand end and beat Stillman twice with his opening deliveries, both perfect outswingers. Unfortunately the blood was rising with each play and miss and Len was cussing audibly. The third delivery was edged just short of third slip, whereupon Lenny completely lost it, unloaded a volley of sledges at the bemused Stillman, charged back to his mark and embarked on a battery of bouncers. At the end of that first over Victoria were 0–20 with Stillman twenty not out, courtesy of three hooks and two square cuts.

Len's great mate was Jeff Thomson. They were both suspended from District cricket once for arriving two hours late for the start of a match, with girlfriends in hand, having been surfing. Their defence was that the surf had been too good to leave! These two didn't get their priorities all that right in the early days. I roomed with Thommo on the 1977 tour of England but really it was like having Lenny as a third room-mate. Every time there was a knock at the door it was 10–1 on to be Len rather than room service. Reception should have issued him with his own key—it would have saved time getting up to open the door!

Lenny's other great mate was Ian 'Wizard' Davis, a tall, upright stroke maker who arrived from Nowra, New South Wales, as a boy wonder in the early '70s. Alas just fifteen Tests were not testimony to Wizard's skill nor was a batting average of 26.61. It was generally agreed that his placid nature was not suited to the tough grind of Test cricket, but perhaps if senior players of the day had treated him more maturely it may have brought a greater return from this most gifted of opening batsmen. The naive psychology of the time was to treat Wizard like the apprentice, to take him out and get him on the drink, to hold him down in the dressing-room and fart in his face. This ongoing pattern of patronising the youngster did him no favours and Wizard drifted out of the game with a reputation as one who didn't realise his full potential.

Another of my era for whom I have great affection was Bruce Francis, an opening batsman who came from the Waverley Cricket Club in Sydney and played just three Tests in 1972. He was intelligent and could bat aggressively. Unfortunately, Bruce did not enjoy the best of relationships with Ian Chappell and it had a profound effect on his enthusiasm for cricket at Test level. Bruce did himself no favours by openly admitting he didn't enjoy fielding and he was a lazy worker at the nets. A chronic sufferer of migraines in an era that didn't understand this most debilitating condition, he was more or less told to take a powder for his headache whenever an attack occurred. He had two seasons with Essex in 1971 and 1972 and scored prolifically for that county. He won the admiration of the Essex dressing-room, appreciated their respect and scored hundreds of runs for them as a result. He was another I felt with better handling would have achieved more.

Bruce's opening partner at the time was Alan 'Fitteran' Turner, an accountant who became an executive with WD & HO Wills. Fitteran played fourteen Tests and averaged just under thirty. He was a hard-hitting left-hander who was as brave as any man of his era. A wholehearted trier in the field, he was my short leg in Test and interstate cricket. Fitteran wore many blows by getting in close in that position. He took a number of bat-pad chances off me and was always eager to get in and work hard for the inside edge via the pad. He was another who probably should have played more at

Alan 'Fitteran' Turner, a hard-hitting accountant, was also a brave short leg who took a number of bat-pad catches off my bowling

the highest level, but when he was omitted from the 1977 tour of England he decided that his future lay in the corporate world, and now holds a strong position with the tobacco company which employed him then. He's fondly remembered for his rolling eyes and his uncomplicated outlook on the game.

Dave Colley, a kindly soul who was affectionately known throughout cricket circles as 'Fox', was the all-rounder for New South Wales in the '70s. This naturally gifted cricketer was something of a Hooray Henry who worked in advertising and would occasionally arrive at Blues training with lunchtime wine on his breath. Again, he played only three Tests for Australia taking six wickets with his fast medium bowling, but he could bat in the lower order and, as a former baseballer, could smite the ball a country mile. Fox was an amateur in a developing

All-rounder David Colley, known around the traps as 'Fox', was an amateur in a developing professional world. He could smite the ball a country mile

professional world. He enjoyed getting away on tour and relaxing. He was not hard-nosed enough to be a major player in his era, but he was possibly fortunate that he was around then because the modern game would have been too professional with too many restrictions on and off the field. Everybody liked Fox and enjoyed playing with him.

Another person of interest from my era was John Gleeson, the mystery spinner from Tamworth. 'Cho', which is short for cricket hours only, was my first room-mate on tour and didn't say much. He played twenty-nine Tests and took ninety-three wickets. He's now closing on seventy years of age. John was known for his folded finger grip. He bowled off spinners but then folded the middle finger of his bowling hand and propelled leg breaks in the Jack Iverson mould. He was a real problem for those who hadn't

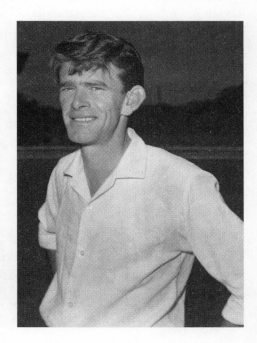

'Cho' (short for cricket hours only) is traditional Australian country. Not big on in-depth conversation, he winkled out the best batsmen (Sir Garfield Sobers three times) with his mystery deliveries

faced that sort of delivery and bemused many a batsman. Barry Richards, the great South African, was initially flummoxed by him. However, he picked him after not too many confrontations; if the fingers were flat the ball was an off break, but if he saw two or three fingers raised upright above the ball it would be the finger-flicking leggie. Some batsmen never read his peculiar grip.

Cricket Australia wants Gleeson to spend time at the Cricket Academy with its coaching staff. The mysteries of folded-finger bowling are still of tremendous interest to senior coaches in the Australian system. A majority of our finger spinners haven't got a doosra and Gleeson's leg break is seen as something akin to this quirky delivery. However, Gleeson remains a very private man. He lives in Tamworth, in full retirement, playing lawn bowls with distinction and drinking most afternoons at the Tamworth City Bowling Club. So far he has rejected every overture to come to the Academy. The fear at Cricket Australia is that he will die with the secrets in him and given that he smokes like a chimney and weighs about fifty kilograms, the time to get him to the Academy is now. Heh, heh, heh!

Cho is a dear old thing, he's traditional Australian country. He isn't big on in-depth conversations and I don't think throughout our playing time together we ever discussed spin bowling. During matches Cho would sit in a hot bath reading the newspapers, a cigarette dangling from his lips. He'd only emerge when it was his time to bat. He never really appeared to watch the game at all, and didn't seem interested in batting or fielding too much. His role was to winkle people out with his mystery deliveries and he did this pretty successfully. In Test cricket he dismissed the great English opening batsman Geoff Boycott on six occasions and claimed the even greater Sir Garfield Sobers three times—pretty impressive notches on a bowler's belt!

Another player of my era with whom I've had contact is the former Test opening batsman, Rick McCosker, a shy, retiring, self-effacing man who was as brave as all get out. He was variously known as 'Rick the Snick' or 'Rick the Rock' depending on whether he was edging the opponents bowlers to the slip cordon or holding them out for hour after hour. Rick hailed from Inverell and was a late maturer, having played for a number of years for the Sydney cricket club on a minefield of a pitch at Rushcutters Bay, but managing to pile on hundred after hundred. Ian Chappell respected him greatly. I roomed with him on occasion.

Rick McCosker, another shy, self-effacing character, was as brave as all get out. This iconic photograph shows him returning to face the music after Englishman Bob Willis broke his jaw during the 1977 Centenary Test in Melbourne

He made a great cup of tea and felt that a steak and vegetables was a meal to be consumed over two hours. He could take forty-five minutes to eat a bowl of cornflakes. Rick liked to chew on his food. He's now a successful financial planner in Newcastle. He and Meryl, his wife of almost thirty years, always warm your heart when you see them at the odd function. Rick was a practising Catholic during the fast and furious '70s—an odd man out to a certain extent but one who was respected for his values nevertheless.

I don't see enough of my former team-mates. That's possibly my fault. I should have worked more at friendships than I did. But most cricketers don't—you play with players and you move on. Football tends to breed stronger bonds for some reason and I'm not sure what it is. Maybe players in the modern era—because they live so closely together for such a long time—will have friendships for life. I think it's a good thing.

THE POMS—2009 ASHES FAVOURITES?

An English friend rang me this morning and declared that his country will regain the Ashes in 2009. The Poms sometimes say the damnedest things. His logic is based on what he saw over five straight nights watching the Second Test match between England and the West Indies at Headingley in England. It sounds poppycock to me. But I notice the highlights package of the Test match is on Fox, and so I intend making a forensic examination of his preposterous declaration.

I cautioned my friend that any form shown against the West Indies in their current parlous state is a little misleading. But he insists there are certain jigsaw pieces in the England line-up now securely in place to knock off the cocksure Aussies who will be without Warne, McGrath and Langer, and quite possibly Gilchrist, and one or two others. Still, I'll sit back and watch two hours of the highlights and that should provide some insights.

Mind you, beating the Windies these days is as easy as buying Lindsay Lohan a drink.

England has won the toss and is batting. We're in deep Yorkshire territory. The First Test was drawn, rain ruining a very strong position for England. They look the more powerful team and winning the toss would seem to be an advantage at Leeds. The West Indies new ball attack is spearheaded by one Daren Powell, a former spinner who has crossed to the dark side to bowl pace. His is a very pragmatic bowling action. He's moving it away from the left-hander Andrew Strauss and his partner Alastair Cook. Strauss averages forty-two in Test cricket. That seems about right as there are certain limitations to his game. There may be a touch of Kepler Wessels, a little bit of Mark Taylor, but there's also something in his technique that says he's not among the elite. His partner Cook could be important to England's future—compact and with a wide stroke range he is going to open for them for a long time.

Strauss is a very fine square cutter and before too long he's offered a juicy pie outside off stump (short and wide) which he despatches past gully to the boundary. Bowling at this level is all about precision and the West Indies is serving up the most imprecise offerings. Glenn McGrath would have shaken his head off his neck if he'd been a party to this load of dross. Eventually, however, Strauss cuts at one that's a little too full and edges to the wicket-keeper. The square cut is his favourite shot and occasionally your pet stroke is a source of betrayal.

Michael Vaughan comes in at number three. He's averaging forty-two in sixty-five Tests which is not too shabby, though he hasn't played for a while. Both Englishmen are good pullers of

Michael Vaughan played with some of his former fluency; neat deflections in symphony with powerful shots all round the wicket

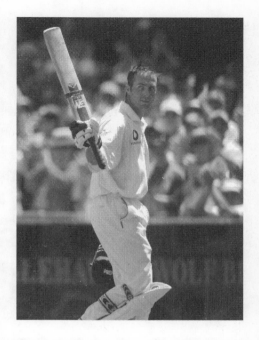

the ball and the West Indies are offering just too much short of a length. Spinner Gayle comes on and, despite his casual, cool relaxed action, produces a peach to win an lbw decision against Cook.

Kevin Pietersen strides to the wicket. He averages fifty in twenty or so Test matches. This is a crucial partnership. Vaughan is stroking beautifully through extra cover and is very good off his pads as well. When I've seen him in the last twelve months I've thought him a shadow of the player who scored so heavily in Australia a few years ago. But this is vintage Vaughan today and there are neat deflections in symphony with powerful shots all around the wicket.

Pietersen can look vulnerable when the ball moves away from him and his hands get right out in front of his body, but the West

Indians are honing in on middle and leg stump so his on-driving has been particularly hurtful. The score is rapidly closing on 200 and the English supporters are in full voice. Just when I thought Ricky Ponting the best on-driver in the modern game, along comes Pietersen to challenge him. His technique of getting the head just outside the line of the ball, checking the shot so that the bottom hand doesn't screw it towards mid wicket, is delighting me from the comfort of my armchair. The former South African is going to serve his adopted country for around a decade, and given that he already averages fifty it would not surprise if he leaves the game with a Test batting average in the mid to high fifties.

The West Indians are struggling to contain the English pair, and Vaughan has his sixteenth Test hundred when he edges nervously past a vacant second slip. Pietersen gives him a full

It's always action packed when Kevin Pietersen's at the crease. His Spice Girl lookalike girlfriend applauded each milestone as he approached his first Test double hundred. Shades of Imran Khan ...

embrace, only just stopping short of nibbling his ear. The cameras cut to the English balcony where players are applauding above heads. The popular captain was much missed during the Ashes of 2006–07. Having reached his hundred Vaughan falls, caught very well on the boundary at deep backward square. At 3–254 England are well placed.

Paul Collingwood comes in averaging forty-four in twenty-two Test matches. 'Colly' is seen as something of a nicker, yet his outside edges are flying past gully for boundaries, and when the bowlers err on the short side Pietersen is all too willing to punish them over mid wicket. Pietersen's bat pick up is technically pure and, while he's looking to get on the front foot, he can still rock back and pull anything centimetres short high over deep mid wicket. He brings up a brilliant century with a delicate leg glance. Collingwood embraces the South African and the dressing-room is again on its feet. Pietersen is such an entertainer.

Collingwood is missed at first slip—when you are in the slips cordon and Colly is on strike and the ball is moving around, you know you've a better than even money chance of being offered an outside edge. And on cue, within an over or so, Colly offers up again and this time it's gratefully accepted by Gayle at first slip off Collymore.

Another English batsman averaging in the mid forties at Test level is Ian Bell, and at twenty-five he is about to enter a period where his powers should be near their peak. He has gained a reputation as a slicer of deliveries which leave him through the air, and Collymore's outswinger accounts for him virtually straight away.

At 5–329 Matthew Prior, shaven headed, belligerent, and with a birth certificate that says Johannesburg Women's Hospital,

England's would-be tilt at regaining the Ashes in 2009 relies heavily on the maturing skills of batsmen like Alastair Cook and Ian Bell. Warney looks unimpressed by something ...

appears. He is fresh from a brilliant century at Lord's, the first England wicket-keeper to score a Test hundred on debut, and appears to be the number seven England has been seeking for years. He's into stride immediately, spearing a drive through mid wicket, a shot reminiscent of Ponting at his best.

At stumps on day one Pietersen is 130 not out, Prior thirteen, and the total 5–366 from just eighty-five overs. England is powering and the deficiencies in West Indian bowling are all too obvious.

Next day Pietersen's fourth Test score of 150 is achieved. His girlfriend is applauding his highest Test score—she looks like one of the Spice Girls and I marvel at the wide range of women modern-day cricketers attract. Prior is hooking and driving when they give him width. His half-century has come off seventy-two balls. Incidentally, Prior's temperament cannot be a problem—he is known in to have locked horns with Shane Warne in a sledging battle, and that takes bottle.

Eventually Prior plays down the wrong line to a good 'un, a late outswinger which squared him up and took the top of middle stump. The wicket-keeper/batsman nodded approval to the bowler and Powell on his way to the pavilion.

Despite the total closing on 500 the West Indians look very buoyant. There are smiles in the cold, and wickets are wholeheartedly celebrated. David Moore has replaced Bennett King as their coach. Moore is a former wicket-keeper from the Sutherland Shire in Sydney who came up through the Australian Cricket Academy coaching system. I knew his father Bob, a kindly soul who loved the game and raised David to share his passion for cricket. David is obviously respected by the team, a difficult thing for an outsider.

Pietersen now has a double century, his first in Test cricket, with twenty-two boundaries. His dig has contained no sixes, which is curious as he loves to go aerial. Peter Moores, the new England coach, must be delighted. The cameras catch his beaming smile as his best batsman continues to fire.

A number of the West Indians have the top buttons on their cricket shirts done up, a sure sign that they're feeling the cold and that their minds are not as concentrated as they should be. This is a look best reserved for Cambridge and Oxford in a pre-season friendly. I've never done the top button on my cricket shirt up; I'd have felt I should also put on a tie.

Pietersen's epic comes to an end when he skies to deep cover and is out for 226 off the persevering Bravo, whereupon Vaughan declares at 7–570. Conditions look bleak but the West Indian cause even bleaker.

The West Indies begins their chase. Gayle is at the top of the order, averaging thirty-nine in Test cricket, with Daren Ganga, who is seen as a potential captain but averages just twenty-eight in limited appearances. They are confronted by Ryan Sidebottom, who played a Test a few years ago without distinction. He's a left-arm over the wicket swing bowler who gets it to curve into the right-hander and away from the left. Ryan is long haired and chunky. I played against his father Arnie, a lively medium fast bowler and hard hitter in the '70s. Arnie combined football with cricket and seems to have sired a very good English prospect. It's been seventy-eight matches between his son's first and second Tests, and although Ryan's not fast at eighty-one miles per hour, anybody who can move it around from that angle, particularly both ways, can cause problems. Gayle is looking in good touch, driving Sidebottom back past mid-off for an early boundary and then whipping him through mid wicket for another. With the total on seventeen Sidebottom gets one to swing back into Gayle and traps the left-hander in front. Gayle is displeased with the decision but 'hawkeye' says it would have clipped leg stump. Clever bowling!

Devon Smith is number three, the most prestigious position in any team's order. The West Indian hierarchy regards him as the leading batsman in their next few years' campaigns. Suddenly Sidebottom has a second wicket—Ganga is dismissed not offering a shot to one that comes back through the air from outside off

Devon Smith's rated highly by
the West Indian selectors, and
he looks the real deal

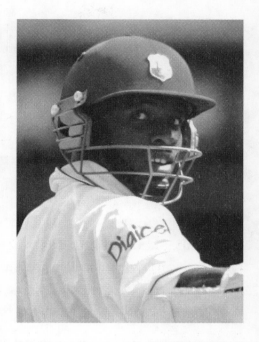

stump. In recent times many have argued that old-fashioned swing bowlers will get a lot of wickets, and I couldn't agree more. Sidebottom is making the ball deviate; changing the path of the ball has worked for a couple of centuries and it shows no sign of becoming passé.

Sylvester Joseph is in at number four. He's another with only a handful of Tests behind him. Steve Harmison is bowling fast from the other end, but Smith is given width and celebrates with a boundary. It's big Harmy's waywardness that's cost him over the years. Smith is again prominent against Sidebottom when he clouts him through cover and West Indies has raced to fifty-one, but has lost two key wickets. Smith looks the real deal, his straight driving is a sure indication of a class player.

Suddenly Harmison strikes with a quicker one and Joseph, driving expansively with feet nowhere, edges to first slip where Strauss holds a chest-high catch. Runako Morton replaces Joseph—he averages twenty-four from just eight Tests and at the age of twenty-eight needs to secure his place soon. The compact Smith is looking in the best of touch as another straight drive off Harmison races to the boundary. Then Cook catches him in the gully as he slices Plunkett off a stiff front leg—you've got to play lower in England, son!

Bravo is at the crease at number six—it's very obvious the West Indies without Lara has real problems. Harmison has Morton taken by Prior behind the stumps off an inside edge, a most athletic piece of wicket keeping, yet some of his work has been shabby and the newcomer will have to improve his general

Ryan Sidebottom's unkempt hair rises to the occasion as he savours the moment. Seventy-eight matches passed between his first and second Test, and he picked up eight wickets second time around

glove work to avoid further scrutiny. Morton is not too happy with the umpire's decision, but takes it like a man and walks proudly off. He has seemingly been dealt a bad card but not overreacted.

Ramdin is in at 5–82 and after hitting Plunkett high over cover he edges to Prior in the very next over. Powell joins the action. Bravo is playing some delightful strokes. From all reports he's Brian Lara's best mate and they've been inseparable on tours. He plays with a West Indian flourish and is finding the rope frequently. Another outswinger produces a catch to second slip, and this time it's Collingwood accepting Powell's full stroke. Plunkett is making the ball bend away from the right-hander from his conventional front-on action, and the English are exploiting the favourable conditions very well indeed.

At 7–115 Sidebottom's back and although only bowling at seventy-seven miles an hour he's still making the ball leap nastily from just short of a good length. Some will judge he lacks that extra yard of pace to be truly effective against teams as strong as Australia, but if he gets suitable conditions Sidebottom could be a handful when Ponting's team defends the Ashes in England in 2009. He looks to have a cheery disposition and, although slightly scruffy looking, he could just be the uncomplicated, hardworking medium pacer that England have a habit of producing.

Bravo's innings ends with the total on 124 when Sidebottom gets one to duck in and clip leg stump. It's a quality piece of bowling and the West Indies is in disarray. The seamers have dominated the day and the Honourable Monty Panesar hasn't had any work. Collymore is taken by Strauss at widish first slip off

Sidebottom and the West Indian innings is over at 142. The follow-on will be enforced with the deficit a massive 424 runs.

Sidebottom is enjoying a tremendous comeback to Test cricket—four first innings wickets, and he again has the new ball late in the day against Gayle and Ganga. Almost immediately wicket-keeper Prior makes a real hash of a straightforward catch off Gayle. This deficiency will have to be addressed. His hands, even to my untrained eye, seem to be at a very strange angle to the ball most of the time. With great glovemen like Ian Healy the ball disappears into the gloves like some vanishing act. Sidebottom is squaring the West Indian batsmen up with his late swing—Ganga falls across the crease, is struck on the pads, and is plumb lbw. A pearler—there's more to Ryan Sidebottom than unkempt hair.

Powell comes in as nightwatchman averaging just seven. I reckon you've got to be averaging at least fifteen to be a nightwatchman. Surviving the day calls for a lot more skill than Powell's with the cue, and offering no shot to a Sidebottom inswinger he becomes the second lbw decision of the second innings. Sidebottom has six wickets for the day.

The highlights package has now rolled into the third day and the commentators are discussing how the temperature has plummeted to seven degrees, although England won't find it too difficult. However, the West Indians will feel unloved by Mother Nature and may not be able to dig themselves out of their grave situation.

Devon Smith has reached the wicket and as he did in the first innings looks impressive, playing late and working through cover off a half front foot. However, Gayle is the key, and straight away

Plunkett has him edging to Prior, who this time takes a very good low catch to his left. Both Prior and Plunkett are enjoying a few good days at Test level. Plunkett is relishing actually playing: in Australia his work load was reduced to bowling at a stump in the middle of Test grounds prior to play beginning each morning. This time he's involved during office hours.

It's 3–37 but Smith continues to hit boundaries through the off side. Sylvester Joseph at the other end has fallen across his stumps and missed a straight one. Both Joseph and Morton look short of genuine Test quality. It's alright to give youth opportunity, but there's something about this pair's techniques that suggests cutting it against the better teams in Test cricket may be a bridge too far. Sidebottom strikes again, this time it's Smith who offers a limp bat to an outswinger and is taken by Strauss at first slip. The diminutive number three is unhappy with the shot, is out for sixteen, and it's 5–57, still a huge deficit of 367 runs.

Dwayne Bravo is at the crease. He averages thirty-three in Test cricket and has more scope than Joseph and Morton. He plays off both feet and is positive. Morton and Bravo are hitting boundaries in a lost cause, and their stroke range is extensive— on-drives, clips through mid wicket. But then Harmison comes on and is immediately rewarded when Morton plays an ill-judged hook shot and Prior runs forward and takes an athletic catch. Harmy is the muscle England needs because he can upset batsmen. Bravo hits Panesar 100 yards and over the long-off boundary to race into the forties. He's a strong striker who plays shots whatever the scoreboard says, and would have been valuable in the strong West Indian teams of the '80s, bowling a bit and batting aggressively in the mid to latter order. To emphasise the point, a hook shot off Harmison brings him his eighth Test fifty, and fourth against England, but at 6–136 the West Indies is going down well inside the distance.

Next Ramdin is struck on the pads by a real shooter from Harmison, and with the temperature still in single figures he departs—his score of five almost matches the thermometer. Panesar now takes his first wicket of the match, the eighth of the second innings, when Bravo races down the pitch and swipes to mid-off. Panesar is the perfect foil for an in-form pace attack.

Corey Collymore comes in. It's such a lovely name and he looks a pleasant fellow. Then Taylor under edges Harmison into his stumps, and with the injured Sarwan unable to bat the West Indies has twice been dismissed in the Test for under 150 runs.

Corey Collymore picked up a couple of middle-order wickets, but they literally cost him a ton of runs

And so England enjoyed a most emphatic victory by an innings and 224 runs. Michael Vaughan produced a brilliant century, Sidebottom added an extra dimension with the new ball, and Prior at number seven seemed a perfect fit. And, of course, there was Pietersen, possibly the premier batsmen in world cricket—with the exception of a couple of Australians.

My verdict at the end of the highlights' package? England is beginning to look like a good team, and with Flintoff returning after injury, and 2009 not that far away, perhaps my friend's preposterous declaration that the Poms have a real chance of reclaiming the Ashes is not such poppycock after all.

England v. West Indies
West Indies in England 2007 (2nd Test)

England first innings		Runs	Balls	Mins	4s	6s
AJ Strauss	c Ramdin b Powell	15	27	35	2	–
AN Cook	lbw b Gayle	42	76	120	2	–
*MP Vaughan	c Morton b Taylor	103	173	235	11	–
KP Pietersen	c Taylor b Bravo	226	262	432	24	2
PD Collingwood	c Gayle b Collymore	29	44	59	3	–
IR Bell	c Ramdin b Collymore	5	12	15	1	–
+MJ Prior	b Powell	75	99	156	9	–
LE Plunkett	not out	44	48	46	7	–
SJ Harmison	did not bat					
RJ Sidebottom	did not bat					
MS Panesar	did not bat					
Extras (1 b, 15 lb, 6 nb, 9 w)		31				

Total (7 wickets, declared, 552 minutes, 122.3 overs) 570

Fall of wickets: 1–38 (Strauss, 8.1 ov), 2–91 (Cook, 26.6 ov), 3–254 (Vaughan, 60.2 ov), 4–316 (Collingwood, 71.5 ov), 5–329 (Bell, 75.2 ov), 6–489 (Prior, 110.3 ov), 7–570 (Pietersen, 122.3 ov)

West Indies bowling	Overs	Mdns	Runs	Wkts	Wides	No-Balls
Powell	33	5	153	2	3	1
Collymore	29	1	110	2	1	2
Taylor	22	4	116	1	–	1
Bravo	24.3	3	97	1	1	1
Gayle	14	1	78	1	–	1

West Indies first innings		Runs	Balls	Mins	4s	6s
CH Gayle	lbw b Sidebottom	11	17	19	2	–
D Ganga	lbw b Sidebottom	5	17	28	–	–
DS Smith	c Cook b Plunkett	26	37	58	4	–
SC Joseph	c Strauss b Harmison	13	37	42	2	–
RS Morton	c Prior b Harmison	5	13	17	–	–
DJ Bravo	b Sidebottom	23	42	69	4	–
+D Ramdin	c Prior b Plunkett	6	15	13	1	–
DBL Powell	c Collingwood b Plunkett	8	15	21	1	–
JE Taylor	not out	23	23	42	4	–
CD Collymore	c Strauss b Sidebottom	3	12	19	–	–
*RR Sarwan	absent hurt					
Extras (13 lb, 6 nb, 4 w)		23				
Total (all out, 168 minutes, 37 overs)		146				

Fall of wickets: 1–17 (Gayle, 4.5 ov), 2–23 (Ganga, 6.2 ov), 3–68 (Joseph, 16.2 ov), 4–74 (Smith, 17.6 ov), 5–82 (Morton, 20.1 ov), 6–94 (Ramdin, 23.1 ov), 7–114 (Powell, 27.4 ov), 8–124 (Bravo, 32.5 ov), 9–146 (Collymore, 37 ov)

England bowling	Overs	Mdns	Runs	Wkts	Wides	No-Balls
Sidebottom	12	2	42	4	–	–
Harmison	12	0	55	2	1	3
Plunkett	12	1	35	3	3	3
Panesar	1	0	1	0	–	–

West Indies second innings (following on)		Runs	Balls	Mins	4s	6s
CH Gayle	c Prior b Plunkett	13	30	50	1	–
D Ganga	lbw b Sidebottom	9	23	29	1	–
DBL Powell	lbw b Sidebottom	0	10	11	–	–
DS Smith	c Strauss b Sidebottom	16	23	40	2	–
SC Joseph	lbw b Sidebottom	1	14	19	–	–
RS Morton	c Prior b Harmison	25	62	78	3	–
DJ Bravo	c Plunkett b Panesar	52	74	94	7	1
+D Ramdin	lbw b Harmison	5	20	20	–	–
JE Taylor	b Harmison	0	2	6	–	–
CD Collymore	not out	0	0	1	–	–
*RR Sarwan	absent hurt					
Extras (1 b, 14 lb, 5 nb)		20				
Total (all out, 178 minutes, 42.1 overs)		141				

Fall of wickets: 1–20 (Ganga, 6.5 ov), 2–22 (Powell, 8.6 ov), 3–30 (Gayle, 11.2 ov), 4–47 (Joseph, 16.1 ov), 5–57 (Smith, 18.1 ov), 6–120 (Morton, 34.5 ov), 7–141 (Ramdin, 40.5 ov), 8–141 (Bravo, 41.6 ov), 9–141 (Taylor, 42.1 ov)

England bowling	Overs	Mdns	Runs	Wkts	Wides	No-Balls
Sidebottom	15	4	44	4	–	–
Plunkett	8	1	25	1	–	1
Harmison	13.1	3	37	3	–	4
Panesar	6	1	20	1	–	–

Source: Courtesy of cricketarchive.com

SLEDGING—AN OVERRATED ART

I'm on the train speeding towards the city from Hurstville. It's 7 am. I can't believe how few conversations happen in trains. My head is not full of conversation. I have to deliver a breakfast address to a hospital administrators' conference. Should be a ball of fun! The coordinator of the two-day event has asked me to include in my delivery a succession of funny sledges that I've heard on the cricket field. I don't know that there has been an oversupply of amusing sledges. There've been quirky comments, and the odd pointed aside, but as for downright, fall-down-grab-the-grass, stop-it-you're-killing-me comedy, there ain't too much. I'm scribbling down as many comments as I can from my career. Here is a cross section.

'I want you to bat as if your life depended on it.' Australian skipper Greg Chappell after telling me of his wish that I open the batting in the second innings of the Centenary Test against England in Melbourne in 1977. My reply was, 'No problems.'

I don't know why I said that as there were plenty of problems and my actual life did depend on how well I managed the job! I ended up scoring 14. It was the toughest fourteen I ever scored.

'Doing too much. Heh, heh, heh!' English umpire David 'Chopper' Constant during a county match in 1972 on why he had turned down my lbw appeal. (Taking the piss out of how much I actually spun the ball.)

'Catch it, Cracker!' Second slip Gary Gilmour shouting to David 'Cracker' Hourn at mid-on late in the day in poor light at the Sydney Cricket Ground in 1974 during a Sheffield Shield match. Cracker was medically blind and as the ball was flying to the point boundary he was unlikely to catch it moving to his left at mid-on. Hands aloft, eyes skywards, he declared 'Where is it?'

'Come in a few paces. He wouldn't reach you in three hits!' New South Wales hard-drinking skipper Doug Walters to Dave Colley at mid-on, with Western Australia's teetotalling blocker Ric Charlesworth on strike. It is the only recorded sledge made by Walters during his first-class career. I sense Doug didn't quite share Charlesworth's safety-first attitude to batting.

'Two years of National Service took the edge off my batting more than beer and cigarettes!' Room-mate Doug Walters at 3 am on the 1976 tour of New Zealand after numerous heart-to-hearts on reasons why he didn't average higher in Test cricket.

'I thought you could bat!' Volatile NSW paceman Len Pascoe on debut to Queensland's Greg Chappell after rapping him on the gloves with a spiteful bouncer.

'I thought you were supposed to be quick!' Chappell immediately returns serve to Pascoe. Everybody, including the combatants, is chuckling uncontrollably.

'Skull, never hook to get off the mark; you rarely play long innings if that is your opening shot.' Victorian 'Happy Hooker' Keith Stackpole to me after I was dismissed for just three (runs that came from a hook shot) against New Zealand. As recall, 'Stacky' seemed to start every other innings with a hook shot!

'World Series Cricket will last two years and then everything will be back to normal!' Greg Chappell at a team dinner on the 1977 Australian tour of England. Spot on, GC.

'Skull, the reason you don't spin the ball is that your finger joints are not lubricated enough. If you drink more with us, you'll get a lot more turn!' Doug Walters, at a late-night drinking session in Trinidad on the Australian tour of the West Indies in 1973, on the remedy for my inability to bowl a big leg spinner.

The great Doug Walters in his pomp: 'Two years of National Service took the edge off my batting more than beer and cigarettes!'

Bruce Collins, QC, to bowler Len Pascoe: 'I may not be as good at cricket as you, Len, but I'm sure I could beat you at Scrabble!'

'I may not be as good a cricketer as you, Len, but I'm sure I could beat you at Scrabble!' Opening batsman and erudite Sydney QC Bruce Collins to wild man Len Pascoe during a Sydney University and Bankstown club match in 1970. Collins had absorbed a fearful barrage of bouncers and vitriol before his winning retort.

'Hey Warr, you've got as much chance of taking a Test wicket on this tour as I have of pushing a pound of butter up a parrot's arse with a hot needle!' An SCG hillite screamed this to MCC fast bowler John Warr during the 1950–51 Test series. Warr did manage to take a solitary wicket, albeit at a cost of 281 runs.

'You must have been f***in' adopted!' Gordon fast bowler Richard Stobo to Bankstown's Dean Waugh (the third of the four Waugh brothers) during a club match in the 1990s. The remark came after Waugh had been beaten four balls in a row by a frustrated Stobo.

'Forget the dead, attend the wounded!' I shouted as team-mates ran to check on the condition of Alan 'Fitteran' Turner and Jeff 'Two Up' Thomson after the two had collided attempting a catch during the Australia–Pakistan Test match at the Adelaide Oval I 1976. Turner was prostrate on the ground, motionless, limp. Thomson was nonchalantly standing clutching his shoulder. Fitteran later complained of a mild headache whereas Two Up's shoulder-blade had snapped in half. Opening batsmen are such wusses!

'The Hampshire opening batsman Barry Richards and Gordon Greenidge make their way to the middle to begin the day's play. Richards is the one in the cap!' The Southampton ground

Opening for Hampshire with Barry Richards, dynamic West Indies opener Gordon Greenidge was the victim of this foolish announcement: 'Richards is the one in the cap!'

announcer over the loudspeaker. Nice one, Captain Obvious! (Richards, of course, is a white South African and Greenidge a black Barbadian.)

'Hold this and count to six. I won't be saying much more to you all day.' Enigmatic leg spinner Stuart MacGill handing his cap to an umpire in a District game. Old Stuie doesn't appear to hold umpires in great regard—doesn't he know that they can make you or break you?

I don't know whether any of these were overly amusing or insightful. I won't touch on sledging at the breakfast. Anyway, it's so overrated.

FRIDAY, 15 JUNE 2007

THE FROG JOKE

I'm at the Sunnyside Tavern in Hamilton, Newcastle, an older-style hotel where patrons of the front bar still wear flannelette shirts and the pub tab does regular business. I'm the guest of the Hamilton Hawks Rugby Club, a strong Catholic-based organisation that plays in the Newcastle–Hunter Valley competition.

Michael Coughlan is the publican and the prime mover behind organising me to address members of the rugby club. I am particularly heartened by the presence of one Gary Gilmour and am struck by how well dear Gus looks. He's drinking diet Coke and hasn't had anything alcoholic for a few years. But he's alive and his new liver appears to be functioning really well.

I'm sitting at my table prior to speaking and Ron Field enquires whether I'm going to tell the frog joke. I say, no. It's not in my repertoire and it's a specific joke for radio cricket. It's amazing the longevity that can accompany certain jokes. I'm still mystified at the success of the only joke I've ever told on air. It was during the third one day international between Sri Lanka and Australia at the Gabba on a working afternoon in March 2006. For the benefit of those who may not have heard the joke here is a transcript:

O'KEEFFE: 'A frog goes into a bank and approaches the teller. He can tell from her nameplate that her name is Patricia Whack. "Miss Whack I'd like to get a $30,000 loan to take a holiday." '

GLEN MITCHELL: 'Bracken to Sangakkara who leaves the ball moving away from him.'

O'KEEFFE: 'Patty looks at the frog in disbelief and asks his name. The frog says his name is Kermit Jagger; his dad is Mick Jagger and it's okay, he knows the bank manager. Patty explains that he will need to secure the loan with some collateral. The frog says sure, I have this, and he produces a tiny porcelain elephant about an inch tall, bright pink and perfectly formed.'

GLEN MITCHELL: [To O'Keeffe] 'Is this going to take many overs?
    'Bracken running away from us again. Sangakkara another leave.'

O'KEEFFE: 'Very confused, Patty explains that she'll have to consult with the bank manger and disappears into the back office. She finds the manager and says, "There's a frog called

239

Kermit Jagger out there who claims to know you. He wants to borrow $30,000 and use this as collateral." She holds up the tiny pink elephant, "I mean what in the world is this?".'

'The bank manager looks back at her and says, "It's a knick-knack, Patty Whack, give the frog a loan, his old man's a rolling stone".'

GLEN MITCHELL: 'Bracken to Sangakkara and he pushes to mid-off, no run.'

Of course, the last part of the joke is told with Glen and me falling about during the punch line. It is an anecdote that is really dependent on a ball-by-ball commentator running with it and not punctuating it with anything as rude as the fall of a wicket. I was lucky. Some people still say to me that that joke went for overs, when, in fact, it went for three deliveries!

Radio is all smoke and mirrors. I will probably never tell another joke on ABC Radio, basically because I haven't got one! I am humbled by everybody's enjoyment of the frog joke and it appears that I will be forever remembered for it.

SATURDAY, 24 JUNE 2007

A TOUGH DAY AT
EAGLE FARM

I've woken up in Brisbane. It wasn't a good night. I'm remorseful. During the week Jim Maxwell and I have been speaking at ABC Grandstand functions in Townsville and Rockhampton. These evenings have involved a little bit of trivia, some quizzes and a lot of fun. Financially it's been worthwhile. I'll be taking home, after tax, around $2000. I'm happy with that. A good week's work! However, the week's wages have been burnt after one solitary hit out overnight.

On the previous evening I caught up with Gary Considine, a fellow I met on my tour of South Africa last year. Gary's done well on the land just out of Toowoomba. He likes a Bundy and Coke and cricket and, more particularly, likes to punt. After a few beers we find ourselves at the Treasury Casino in Queen Street. Gary's playing blackjack and I pull up a chair next to him. Initially we're betting in $10.00 chips. Suddenly things start to escalate. Within half an hour they're out of control. I'm losing and he suggests a change of table. We go to the roulette. I've never played roulette. Suddenly I'm having $200 on things without any system, without any rhyme or reason. At 1 am I shake Gary warmly by the hand outside the Treasury Casino and stumble back to my hotel. I've worked the week in North Queensland for nothing. My take-home pay when I return to my loving wife will be zilch.

It's Saturday, there is a get out: I have all day to myself before the fundraiser tonight. I decide to head off to Eagle Farm races and work my betting system. I've never been to that noble thoroughbred raceway. I have coffee and look at the form and all the qualifiers. Interstate races are at Randwick, Mooney Valley and Morphettville. At Eagle Farm there aren't many options around the odds I want to wager at, plus Eagle Farm never returns too much. There is only one qualifier at Randwick. It's in the first and it's called Bolombi Road, but it will be around $15.00 and the race is at 10.40 am local time. I'm not getting to the track that early. I'm desperate, but don't want to be seen to be *that* desperate.

Mooney Valley is the Victorian meeting. It's my least favourite for my system and the spread isn't good: there are hurdle and steeple races and I just don't have a good feeling about it. I decide that Morphettville will be my track and I need to make up around $2000. I'm ready. I catch a cab to the racecourse. Wayne, a Kiwi, is my driver. He's a big fan of ABC cricket and we talk warmly about Australia's dominance, how bad the Kiwis have been over the years, and the negativity and the ordinariness of the '70s. He bids me good luck as I depart and head towards the gateway of the racecourse. It's been a $30.00 cab fare, it's another $25.00 to get in, plus $5.00 for a race-card. Fair dinkum, I'm chasing, but I'm already outlaying more to chase.

There's a slight drizzle and it's cold, but there's no colder place than a racecourse when you're on the chase. I don't know anybody. Suddenly I'm tapped on the shoulder by a bright young man in a Queensland Turf Club shirt. It's Sam Clark, a mate of my son Daniel. He's up here working the bar at the winter carnival. His uncle is chairman of the racing club and Sam has been picking up a few bucks before he makes his move into the world of tertiary education. He's a great bloke, though he supports the ACT Brumbies. Still, I'll forgive him for that.

I'm on my way to the betting ring. I decide to look set around the ledger rather than the rounds. There are three main bookmakers: Andrew Adcock, who has stern features but seems to offer the best odds; Graham Tew, who looks conservative and I anxiously note fluctuations; and Murray G Bird. I'm not betting with Murray G on principle. If you work the ledger with a middle initial on your board, you don't deserve patronage.

There aren't many people at the final day of the winter carnival. There's fashion on the field. A number of the ladies have tried—they look nice but they're dressed for thirty-five degrees and it's only ten degrees. The blokes haven't made much of an attempt—I'm in jeans and a duffle coat—even though first prize is a $1295 Paul Barry menswear suit, tie and shirt. I probably should have made the final viewing of those who did.

As a non-smoker it doesn't worry me where they herd the smokers, but at Eagle Farm they're corralled into little fenced sections where they puff away so prominently that people can walk past and comment on their evil habit. They should be given more discreet places to have a puff.

The food is roast beef in the ledger dining area and I tuck in. It's comfort food: I've got no money, but I have a bank and I need to win. I can't return to my family having been away all week working with nothing to show.

The qualifiers for my system from Morphettville look interesting. I decide I'm going to have $200 each way on every horse that qualifies for my system. There's nothing in the first race but the second race, for two-year-olds, has thrown up a horse called Chiche, to be ridden by Dean Yendall, which I'm very interested in backing. However, it's come up at 6–4 and I can only bet if it gets out past 2–1 each way. He's the top weight with 57.5 kilograms but he won at his last start at Morphettville and he raced the previous Saturday. None of the others have any real form, so he's short odds. There's a delay in the start of the race at Mooney Valley. I don't back Chiche because of the odds and naturally enough the horse wins by a short neck.

Race three throws up a horse called Talanto and a beast named Chewy-on-your-Boot. Talanto opens at $29.00 and Chewy-on-your-Boot at $12.00. Unless there's a massive move for Chewy I won't be betting on this race. There's no real move for either and I watch the race. Chewy-on-your-Boot runs boldly to finish a close fourth and I'm really encouraged that my system, which has had the odd good day at Morphettville, could work and regain the lost money.

I speculate on something called Count Henry at the locals—it runs nowhere. I'm further behind. I don't know why I backed the Count. It was a qualifier in my system but Eagle Farm has always given poor returns and it was showing $15.00 anyway.

Now I need $2500 to even come back to wife and children with my head reasonably high. There is nothing in race four at Morphettville but in race five there are three qualifiers, the top weight Irkutsk, the equal top weight Relentlessly, and despised outsider Dekota Gold. Irkutsk is opens at $18.00 and drifts to $20.00. Dekota Gold opens at $17.00 and drifts to $21.00. Relentlessly, however, is solid in the market—it opens at $6.20 and firms into $4.70 before getting out to $5.00. Bookmaker Adcock appears the gambler in the ledger ring, but I'm not taking his skinny odds here. He has my horse under the odds. I'm going to have $300 each way on Relentlessly. I decide to bet on the tote. It looks a touch of overs. I walk into ledger tote and back the horse. Unlike Sydney where tote operators give you a cold stare, Eagle Farm has a friendliness, and the youthful operator says 'Good luck' as he gives me my ticket. I've never had a bookmaker or a TAB worker wish me good luck—it's different here in Brissy! Anyway I'm standing in front of a monitor. I want Relentlessly to win very badly indeed and it's back in the pack as the race unfolds. Matthew Neilson is the hoop and he hasn't ridden the best of races. It's down the outside but Claire Lindop has stolen a march and Relentlessly can do no better than third. Nonetheless, I'm reasonably happy. He pays $2.20 and I have something for my money for my wager. I haven't lost, but I'm still chasing.

Race six is interesting—there are two qualifiers, Son of Spartacus and Tradesmen's Choice. Son of Spartacus opens at $12.00, there'll have to be money for me to be on the Son, and Tradesmen's Choice, again ridden by Matthew Neilson, has opened at $8.00. I'm going to be on the Tradesmen. They're off! I've had another $300 each way—I need the Tradesmen to come in the front entrance. He's back in the pack and Neilson is not riding well—he's five wide on the turn and making some impression. Again Neilson has betrayed me with a poor ride and he makes late ground to finish fourth. Another $600 has jumped out. I'm not happy. I don't care if the Tote operator says good luck all day—there's no point if I'm losing money. I'm now over $3000 behind. This isn't good. There's no lonelier place than a race course when you're on the chase desperate and losing money. I seek more comfort food and drain a big bucket of chips with salt and sauce. There's no conversation with fellow punters, there's very little humour—everybody is chasing a winner.

I bump into Peter Leslie, he played a couple of games for New South Wales in the late 1960s. One tired and emotional night I told him that he could have been Australia's Wasim Akram. He's a good bloke who has retired from a career of school teaching. As a shareholder in a couple of horses in early races at Eagle Farm, he's a little downcast. Neither ran up to expectations, but, we agree, that's racing. I leave him with a promise to catch up next time I'm in the area. He was part of a St George team that I enjoyed playing in back in the '60s and '70s. He tells me my former team-mate, Bruce Francis, has lost twenty-five kilograms and has embarked on a searching fitness campaign. All I want to do is go and have more coffee and chips.

Race seven is my final chance. The only qualifier in the race is a noble steed called Flying Phoenix. This just has to win. It's opened up at a around $7.00. Bookmaker Adcock is offering better odds than the Tote. I'm around $3000 down. I need this thing to win. The Tote is offering $7.70 a win and $2.40 a place. I'm cashed up, but I'm dipping into my reserves. I decide that I'm going to have

$500 each way. It's not death or glory, I've got to walk out of Eagle Farm ahead. Kayla Stra is my hoop. She's a well-performed South Australian rider. Why I'm betting in Morphettville, I don't know. The commentators are saying how unlucky Flying Phoenix was at its last start when it ran third. I don't care about the last start, I want it to have all the luck this start.

They're off. My horse has begun brilliantly but Stra has had to use it up to get to the lead from barrier eleven. I'm in front and on the bit. Oh go you good thing! This is looking promising. They turn. Stra gives the horse a dig in the ribs and he lets down. I'm home. I'm 100 metres out. Uh oh! Here comes a 12–1 shot ridden by Justin Potter called Sweet Julia. Oh no! It's coming late. Hold on for heaven's sake! Stra's getting every inch she can out of my horse. I need this. This is a huge result. Photo! Oh no! Even from my angle on a course monitor at Eagle Farm I sense the worst. Sweet Julia has just pipped my noble beast. Immediately they have a print—there it is beaten by a short half head. I'm on my way home. There are no other qualifiers. I finished square on the day, but still trail after my ill-fated night at the Treasury Casino.

I'm catching a cab home. I seem to be outlaying a lot of money at the moment but it's better than walking. I've got my fundraiser and the company of some coppers tonight. At least I can have a drink because I'm staying at the hotel where the function is, and Ross Musgrove, the Queensland Police Union media heavy will be there. He's always good company.

Oh well, no use whinging. That's the life of the punter. And I must remember—there's no such thing as a last race!

SATURDAY, 7 JULY 2007

HUMPHREY AND BENJI

My wife and younger son are at a surf lifesaving training weekend in Wollongong and my oldest son is working at an eyewear conference in Darling Harbour. I'm at home by myself with my two dogs. The pooches are impatient. They know it's walk time. It's mid-morning and I'm at my desk. I'm preparing to host a function at the Australia versus South Africa Rugby Test at Telstra Stadium that afternoon—a bout of bronchitis has weakened me physically. Dogs don't understand illness. They give me that why-not-Daddy? look and normally I melt. Today is no exception and off we go.

We have two dogs, Benji and Humphrey. Benji's a little sweetheart, a Shitzu Maltese cross, whom we rescued from the pound in September 2005. Benji was found in a park in a cardboard box, wet, matted and flea infested. He's the cutest little boy and the O'Keeffes love him. He's rising six years old and has a very quiet nature, but he can fire up if somebody he doesn't know enters our house. Sadly, he must have been mistreated and

Benji, left, and Humphrey, a delightfully gay couple

denied a childhood. We've tried endlessly to encourage him to chase a ball or run and grab a soft toy between his teeth, but he won't play games.

We've fostered a few dogs over the years and we sensed that Benji needed a companion. My wife keeps an eye on the Paws website for dogs that have been surrendered or rescued, which led us to foster a Lhasa Apso with one eye, named Nelson. Nelson enlivened proceedings at home and drew Benji out of his shell. But the road accident in which he lost his eye had caused some sort of brain damage and he was prone to erraticism. We were pleased when a family decided to adopt Nelson. Unfortunately the adoption didn't work out. He is now with a foster carer in the Blue Mountains where he's apparently fallen in love with horses. With Nelson's departure Benji again lost his *joie de vivre*.

Soon afterwards, though, my wife phoned with news that Humphrey, a Spoodle, was to be our latest foster dog. He'd been surrendered to the pound allegedly for killing three sheep and suffering from anxiety. Four weeks after fostering Humphrey we adopted him.

I came back from the World Cup in the West Indies and within a day had fallen in love with this beautiful Spoodle, so gentle, so happy, and such an ideal companion for Benji. This was an easygoing dog who was relaxed with humans and other animals. The allegation of murdering three sheep was obviously piffle. This guy stepped around grasshoppers on his walks. There's not a mean bone in Humphrey's body.

They make a delightful couple—Benji is black and Humphrey looks like a caramel sheep—and are amusing on their walks: Benji doesn't really get out of a casual shuffle and Humphrey rapturously bounds around with ears flapping and tail wagging.

This day some of my boys' friends are out for a walk. There's Kimmy, a black poodle owned by Carol, a stately woman who travels widely. Benji's always loved Kimmy. We were hoping a relationship, platonic of course, would develop. And it has, to a certain extent, but Humphrey is all over Kimmy like a cheap suit and I sense that the extra enthusiasm of the Spoodle has interested the flirtatious poodle. A further hundred yards along there's Sally, a greyhound. Sally would rather cuddle a lure than pursue it. She's a lovely old thing and quite intrigued with our long-haired Spoodle who embraces her enthusiastically. They sniff each other's behinds endlessly—nothing ever happens, thank goodness—while Benji stands guard next to his mate, just in case there's trouble. I don't know what Benji would do if there was a fracas, but his teeth are like sharp pins.

At home they have their own beds. There have been some reasonably disturbing scenes between them. They kiss a lot. I believe they're just swapping saliva for rehydration purposes, but the contentious issue in my family is whether or not they are gay. I don't think they are. They're confused, without question, and they love each other and, yes, there are just too many open displays of affection. Maybe Humphrey will get over it as he ages. One day I expect Humphrey to come to me and instead of saying, 'Dad, I'm a hairdresser', say, 'Dad, I'm gay.' It's hard to imagine a gay canine hairdresser, but Humphrey has potential nonetheless. I still love the big guy.

THE ENDLESS QUEST
TO BE LIGHTER

We've all been guilty of opening remarks that we'd give anything to have over again. Gobsmackingly innocent starters like 'When are you due?' when the poor girl is simply coming off a two-week, pasta-gorging holiday in Greece.

These days I tend to be more conservative and sensitive with initial remarks. You see, I feel that we can do better than 'Aren't you cold?' or 'Aren't you hot?' depending on how sparse or copious the other party's clothing is in relation to the outside temperature. Imbeciles begin conversations with these kinds of openers. If the thermometer reads minus two degrees Celsius, and someone I know approaches wearing nothing but a T-shirt, stubbies and thongs, I generally lead with, 'Can you get those thongs in blue?'. I reckon it's conversation killing to begin with, 'Aren't you cold?' And why should you go for the easy, boring option, anyway?

The same applies to weight. As someone who has popped the odd kilo on over the last twenty years, I have been the recipient of every old weight-gaining chestnut in the book. You know the ones: 'Gee, Skull, you've been in a good paddock!' or 'Fair dinkum, Skull, have you swallowed a pig?' or that eternal winner, 'How f***ing fat are you?'. Such opening remarks can't take a dialogue anywhere. When will the dimwits realise they are positive conversation killers?

Again, if I bump into an old friend who may be a lazy forty kilos heavier than when I last saw him, my greeting would be something like, 'I like what you've done with your hair'. It's not all that difficult to find a more inspiring lead-in.

Cricketers are just a little too narcissistic for their own good. For us, it's all about the look. More so in retirement, too, I reckon. Reunions or special presentation functions are a nightmare for former players who may be a cheeseburger or two over par. They are derided, spurned and generally spoken ill of. It's absurd. One may have, in his spare time, found a cure for spina bifida, but if he's a little bit of a fatty boom stick that will be the main discussion about him.

Having said all this, I am overweight—not obese (that's my biased observation, anyway)—but at a stage when the simple act of tying my shoelaces can feel like I'm about to give birth. Okay, I tip the scales at 107 kilograms these days. And I want to do something about it; not because of a burning desire to alter the opening remarks. I found out a few years ago that doesn't work. I'd lost a good deal of weight in the mid 1980s and on meeting David Hookes for the first time in a few months, he greeted me with, 'Have you got AIDS, Skull?' So you can't win, either way.

No, my reasons are purely to be able to enjoy as good a quality of life as I can over the remainder of my time.

I recently hosted a rugby union function in Melbourne, and during the evening a middle-aged New Zealander approached and mentioned that his particular talent was reading palms, and could he peruse my right hand. After what seemed an eternity of inspection and multiple 'Umms' and 'Ahhs', my palmist announced that I would enjoy good health till the age of seventy-five, but would encounter real hurdles around seventy-eight or seventy-nine. Doh! I'm fifty-seven, only twenty-odd years to go if I believe this curious Kiwi, who looked as if a stiff cognac would see him out. Late seventies is not enough for this old leg spinner. I want to crack late eighties, say eighty-seven, the cricketer's devil number. How can I achieve it? The only way I know is to cut out eating junk and RUN! And I mean run! Countless kilometres weekly. From this day I plan to be a sort of Forrest Gump. I'm going to run everywhere: to airports, to cricket matches, to get a newspaper. The fittest I've ever been (circa 1975) was achieved by running.

I want to walk into the ABC cricket commentary box for the Australia and India New Year Test match on 2 January 2008 and hear someone say to me, 'Aren't you hot?'. No, sorry, I mean, "Have you been crook?" That is the opening remark opposite of 'You've been eating well over the festive period, Skull.' If my weight starts with an eight in early 2008 I won't care about appropriate conversation starters ever again.

MONDAY, 6 AUGUST 2007

FORBES CUP DAY AND SKULLA CROWNIE'S LAST CHANCE

Forbes is a small western New South Wales town about four hours' drive from Sydney. I'm heading there today to back my horse, Skulla Crownie, in a sprint race on Forbes Cup day. Ben Hall and a few other bushrangers used to knock about around the area and it has an extraordinary number of hotels for such a little community. I've already been to this neck of the woods once or twice, notably to attend a fundraiser for victims of the Bali bombings. The local rugby team, the Forbes Platypi, were on tour in Bali when the terrorists struck and townspeople lost loved ones.

Skulla Crownie is attempting to overcome setbacks and race to his full potential, and I'm going to be there if today is the day. It's all on the line for Skulla, our brave four-year-old gelding. His first two runs, after a 417-day break because of suspensory ligament and chest problems, have resulted in a tenth at Dubbo over 1000 metres and an eleventh of fourteen at Muswellbrook over 1280 metres. Skulla is better than those two runs. Today, however, is D-Day ... he has to show something or six months in the paddock is the alternative.

The journey by car is long, but I've set out early to escape the peak-hour traffic and I'm soon sailing along past Lithgow, Bathurst and Orange. I eventually reach Forbes just as they're loading the horses into the barrier for race one. It's not the best of days. The temperature is hovering around eleven or twelve degrees and there is heavy cloud cover. With his prodigious swing, Zaheer Khan would have bowled teams out by lunch on just such a day.

The first person I see on parking my car is our trainer, Tracey Bartley. The former jockey oversees the campaigns for the stable star, Snipers Bullet. He looks in good spirits, but greets me with, 'Skull, I don't think I'd be backing your horse today'. Not words I wanted to hear, to be perfectly frank. Isn't the trainer supposed to tell you that your horse is special or, at the very least, a good chance each way? I've driven for hours in the hope that his opening remarks would be something like 'Your horse is on fire ... you're going to win plenty on him today.'

On further discussion, Tracey informs me that Skulla just won't stretch out in his track work. He's treated him with the horse chiropractor, but there is something either mental or physical preventing the beast from doing his best. This is sad indeed because when Skulla won his maiden at Narromine in April 2006 a rosy future was predicted for the beautiful crown gelding. Tracey goes on to say that if he were at his best he would win today's race but he has grave misgivings about whether he'll stretch out. I'm not overly fazed by the trainer's remarks. Soon I am in the company of David 'Ringers' Ringland and Alan Marks—two co-owners. We venture to the stalls and there is Skulla Crownie in what looks like the pinkest of conditions. Tracey always turns out his horses in fine fettle … there is no winter coat, Skulla is glistening and I reckon he looks like a winner.

Owners, however, often have a jaundiced view of their horse. Ringers is unconvinced about the way the horse is standing; he feels that he may be favouring his chest because of his splayed feet position. Ringers is a real horseman. He's owned thoroughbreds for years and has an eye far more trained than most. I should be heeding his assessment.

Skulla Crownie is being attended by Shannay, the stable strapper. She's a lovely girl who obviously cares deeply for the animals. I ask what she thinks of Skulla. 'Oh, I love the big guy, but he's just such a sook. I feel so sorry that he's had these setbacks. He's got such a sweet nature, he looks good and he's just great to be around.' That's all I needed to hear. I'm doubling my bet.

Sometimes your heart can rule your head on a racecourse. I'm stroking Skulla's mane and caressing his nose. He's staring at me and I'm reading that he's saying, 'I'm having a crack today, Kerry.' At least I hope that's what he's saying to me.

Skulla is in race four. It's a class one handicap over 1200 metres. First prize is $4900, plus there's also a starters' subsidy of $200 for non-prize-earning runners. At least we'll get two hundred bucks if he runs like a dromedary. The horses are parading. The favourite is Phaeton, trained by Sarah Murray-Leslie of Bathurst. This three-year-old gelding looks good as well. Tracey saw him win a maiden at Gulgong a couple of months before and thought he had a lot of ability, although I don't want to hear *that* from my trainer either. I want him talking about *my* horse. Skulla is to be ridden by Joe Galea. I meet him for the first time and he seems a pleasant enough bloke. He'd already ridden the first winner on the card. Tracey tells Joe that he wants him to jump Skulla and ride him hard into a forward position because in his previous two starts he'd left the barrier sluggishly, costing him any chance of victory. Anyway, I bid Joe a safe journey and good luck. Tracey warns me as we leave the enclosure that he's still not confident about Skulla giving of his best. And I'm still not fazed in the least. I'm out in the betting ring and I've got $500 that says my horse is going to win the race. The biggest bookmaker in the Forbes ring is Hillary Cohen, who lives at Mumbil in the central west. Hillary's not afraid to let you on for any sort of money, and soon my $500 is in his clerk's bag.

I've taken 7–1 and I'm comfortable with the odds. Phaeton is $2.90 favourite and will be hard to beat. I'm in the stands ... they're off. Skulla is tardy again out of the barrier (damn it) and Galea, on instructions, rides him hard to try and take up a position, but the horse is reluctant to go forward. At the 800-metre mark it appears that Galea has him on the bit and, as they swing around the turn, although Skulla's well back in about eighth position in a field of ten, I'm still thinking he can mow them down. In the straight Skulla appears to be knuckling down to his task, but he's still not full gallop. Although he passes some tired horses he can do no better than fifth. Back to the enclosure, where Jockey Galea explains that Skulla just would not give under pressure. I'm not upset, but I'm disappointed because Skulla's problems would appear to be mental, although Ringers assures me there's something wrong with his wither.

We're back at the stalls and strapper Shannay has just hosed Skulla down. Our boy wouldn't blow out a candle—his breathing is as measured as if he'd just completed a morning walk with John Howard. This adds to the frustration as it would appear he had so much more to give. Shannay is cuddling him and I'm cuddling him, trying to convey to him that fifth isn't bad. But our trainer, ever the realist, says that there were a lot of bad horses in the race and he should have finished at least fifth, and on his best form would have won the event. Phaeton, of course, saluted the judge first, and Tracey confides that this horse will win better races.

We're in the bar and Tracey suggests to Ringers, Marksy and me that Skulla Crownie has a rest for six months. So, a spell in the paddock to get over his mental and physical problems is unanimously agreed on, and a return to the racecourse in the New Year roughly planned.

It hasn't been a good day. I've driven five hours, lost my money on my horse, and now I'm chasing. Sadly, this is a familiar position for me on the punt. It has all come down to me having to back the winner of the major event, the Forbes Cup, for the day to be anything like worthwhile. Jockey Galea is on Virtue and Vice, the $3.80 favourite. I've decided that I'm going to bet everything I've got left in my wallet on this 'good thing'. Around the turn and I'm on good terms with myself. Galea has Virtue and Vice poised to run down the leader, On My Honour, ridden by

Miss Brooke McFadden, a 3-kilo claiming girl. That shouldn't be any problem ... Unfortunately it is, and Miss McFadden holds out Virtue and Vice to win by a head.

Broke, disappointed and not looking forward to five hours on the road I head out to the car park. Not surprisingly the journey home seems much longer.

PHOTOGRAPHIC CREDITS

The publisher and author would like to thank the following for permission to reproduce the images throughout this book:

p. 7   © Patrick Eagar
p. 8   © Newspix / News Ltd
p. 13   ABC Archives
p. 19   © Newspix / News Ltd
p. 23   © Sport the library/ Action Photos
p. 30   Photographer: Bruce Long; © Newspix / News Ltd
p. 33   © Patrick Eagar
p. 34   © Patrick Eagar
p. 40   O'Keeffe Family Archives
p. 45   Photographer: Chris Hyde; © Newspix / News Ltd
p. 49   © Patrick Eagar
p. 54   Photographer: AFP/ Alexander Joe; © Newspix / News Ltd
p. 55   Photographer: AFP/ Alexander Joe; © Newspix / News Ltd
p. 57   Photographer: AFP/ Alexander Joe; © Newspix / News Ltd
p. 58   Photographer: AFP/ Alexander Joe; © Newspix / News Ltd
p. 76   © Patrick Eagar
p. 77   (left) ABC Archives; (right) © Newspix / News Ltd
p. 78   Photographer: Mark McCormack; © Newspix / News Ltd
p. 81   Photographer: Phil Hillyard; © Newspix / News Ltd
p. 82   Photographer: Phil Hillyard; © Newspix / News Ltd
p. 83   Photographer: Titus Ray; © Newspix / News
p. 85   Photographer: Phil Hillyard; © Newspix / News Ltd
p. 87   Photographer: Titus Ray; © Newspix / News Ltd
p. 91   Photographer: Phil Hillyard; © Newspix / News
p. 92   Photographer: Phil Hillyard; © Newspix / News Ltd
p. 93   Photographer: Phil Hillyard; © Newspix / News Ltd
p. 101   ABC Archives
p. 103   (top) Photographer: John Feder; © Newspix / News Ltd; (bottom) Photographer: Simon Dallinger; © Newspix / News Ltd

PHOTOGRAPHIC CREDITS